THE INCHON LANDING, KOREA, 1950

Bibliographies of Battles and Leaders

The Battle of Antietam and the Maryland Campaign of 1862: A Bibliography
D. Scott Hartwig

The Central Pacific Campaign, 1943–1944: A Bibliography
James T. Controvich

American Warplanes, 1908–1988: A Bibliography
Myron J. Smith, Jr.

Pearl Harbor: A Bibliography
Myron J. Smith, Jr.

The Battles of Coral Sea and Midway, 1942: A Selected Bibliography
Myron J. Smith, Jr.

The Battle of Jutland: A Bibliography
Eugene L. Rasor

The Falklands/Malvinas Campaign: A Bibliography
Eugene L. Rasor

The Normandy Campaign, 1944: A Selected Bibliography
Colin F. Baxter

The Spanish Armada of 1588: Historiography and Annotated Bibliography
Eugene L. Rasor

General Matthew B. Ridgway: An Annotated Bibliography
Paul M. Edwards

The Pusan Perimeter, Korea, 1950: An Annotated Bibliography
Paul M. Edwards

General Douglas MacArthur, 1880–1964: Historiography and Annotated Bibliography
Eugene L. Rasor

THE INCHON LANDING, KOREA, 1950

An Annotated Bibliography

Compiled by
Paul M. Edwards

Bibliographies of Battles and Leaders, Number 13
Myron J. Smith, Jr., Series Adviser

Greenwood Press
Westport, Connecticut • London

Library of Congress Cataloging-in-Publication Data

Edwards, Paul M.
   The Inchon Landing, Korea, 1950 : an annotated bibliography /
compiled by Paul M. Edwards.
      p.   cm.—(Bibliographies of battles and leaders, ISSN
1056–7410 ; no. 13)
      Includes bibliographical references and index.
      ISBN 0–313–29135–7
      1. Korean War, 1950–1953—Campaigns—Korea (South)—Inchon—
Bibliography.   2. Korean War, 1950–1953—United States—
Bibliography.   3. Korean War, 1950–1953—Bibliography.   I. Title.
II. Series.
Z3319.K6E39   1994
[DS918.2.I5]
951.904′2—dc20   94–10360

British Library Cataloguing in Publication Data is available.

Library of Congress Catalog Card Number: 94–10360
ISBN: 0–313–29135–7
ISSN: 1056–7410

First published in 1994

Greenwood Press, 88 Post Road West, Westport, CT 06881
An imprint of Greenwood Publishing Group, Inc.

Printed in the United States of America

∞™

The paper used in this book complies with the
Permanent Paper Standard issued by the National
Information Standards Organization (Z39.48–1984).

10 9 8 7 6 5 4 3 2 1

CONTENTS

SERIES FOREWORD

The Greeks at Thermopylae, the Crusades, the Armada campaign, Trafalgar, Verdun, Gettysburg, El Alamein, Pork Chop Hill, Khe Sahn, the Falklands, and "Desert Storm" are only a few of the many campaigns and battles, large and small, which have been fought down through the ages. Of course, each of these operations had leaders ranging in quality from Leonidas at Thermopylae to the group think of Vietnam and all featured diverse strategy, tactics, and weaponry. It appears to be mankind's unhappy lot that war has been and apparently will for sometime continue to be a growth industry, despite centuries of horror-filled record-keeping and preventative lessons available for the learning. With only a few exceptions, monographic bibliographies of individual battles and leaders (our series title admittedly, is borrowed from the famous American Civil War history), campaigns and weapons have not been compiled previously. Contributors to this series while thus breaking new ground have also constructed works suitable for wide general audiences. These tools may profitably be employed at every level from high school through graduate university and by the casual researcher/buff as well as the dedicated scholar.

Each volume begins with a narrative overview of the topic designed to place its subject within the context of specific wars, societies, and times; this introduction evaluates the significance of the leader, battle, or technology under study. Each work points to key archival and document collections as well as printed primary and secondary sources. Citations are numbered, allowing easy access via the index(es). Individual volumes may present discussion of their citations in styles ranging from bibliographical essays to individually annotated entries and some titles provide chronologies and suitable appendix(es).

It is my hope as editor that these bibliographies of battles and leaders will enable broad audiences to select and work with the best items available within literature and to benefit from the wisdom of some of today's leading military scholars.

Myron J. Smith, Jr., Series Adviser
Tusculum College
Greeneville, Tennessee

PREFACE

On 25 June, 1950, powerful and well trained troops
of the North Korean People's Army, led by Russian made
T-34 tanks, crossed the 38th parallel and began what
would prove to be one of the more significant wars of
the 20th century. This invasion of the Republic of
South Korea provoked reaction by both the United Nations
and the United States. Soon more than thirty nations
were committed to action in Korea.

The American staffed Korean Military Advisory Group
had remained in Korea after American occupation troops
were withdrawn to Japan in June of 1949. They were
there to train the ROK (Republic of Korea) army to meet
such aggression. But the small army was not large
enough, well enough trained, nor adequately equipped to
stem the tide of the communist forces which forged
across the parallel.

Defeat after defeat followed as the world prepared
for a response. When President Harry Truman committed
the United States to military involvement, General
Douglas MacArthur, as Commander in Chief of the Far
East, was assigned the job of stopping the North
Koreans. The first response, a task force of hastily
collected men, was of little value. Poorly trained and
lacking proper equipment, the courageous men from the
24th Infantry Division were not able to stop the
advance.

The investment of men, machines, and money which

increased during July and August of 1950 did little to
slow the invasion. Trading lives for time, units of the
armies of the United States and Republic of Korea moved
ever south, their defense resting on the shrinking
perimeter around the essential port of Pusan. Locked
there, fighting a series of holding actions, the Eighth
Army under the command of General Walton H. "Bulldog"
Walker, was slowly supplied and reinforced by units from
America and from participating United Nations countries.
     From Douglas MacArthur's first visit to the front
in June of 1950, he had believed that only an amphibious
landing, designed to cut the supply lines of the North
Korean People's Army, could halt the advance and put the
United Nations on the offensive. But his plans for
landing at Inchon met with considerable opposition from
the Joint Chiefs of Staff. Operation Chromite, as it
was finally approved, went forward on 15 September,
1950, when troops of the First Marine Division landed at
Wolmi-do and then at Inchon.
     From every military angle the assault at Inchon,
and the land battle for Seoul, was successful. Landing
with few casualties and moving inland with great speed
the Marines broke the North Korean hold. The Eighth
Army struggled free from the Pusan Perimeter and moved
north. There, joining the men of the First Marines and
the 7th Infantry Division (Army), Seoul was retaken and
the first phase of the Korean War brought to a
successful completion.
     There are several important questions associated
with the Inchon landing. Was the amphibious landing
necessary? Wasn't it possible for the Eighth Army to
break out, especially if Walker had been allowed to
retain the troops withdrawn for the Inchon action? Was
the gamble -- estimated by many to be 5000 to 1 -- too
big a gamble for MacArthur to take? Why did the Joint
Chiefs of Staff give in to MacArthur? Why, when the
North Koreans obviously knew about the landing, were
they so ill prepared to defend this important harbor?
     Often the military aspects of this significant
operation play a distant second to questions about the
controversial leader, General of the Army Douglas
MacArthur. MacArthur was obviously one of the more
significant generals of World War II and was the able

leader in Japan's long road to democracy and recovery.
But his role in the Korean War, and his gamble at
Inchon, were to raise many serious questions.

While historical coverage of the Korean War has
never been strong, with interest far behind that shown
for both World War II and Vietnam, the Inchon campaign
has attracted a large share of what attention is given
the Korean War.

Materials Included

This bibliography covers material dealing with the
Inchon-Seoul campaign. Among Korean War materials the
Inchon landing is one of the most documented campaigns,
for it is an interesting and exciting story. The second
phase of the campaign, the attack along the eighteen
mile front from Inchon to Seoul, was a dirty and costly
battle. Joined by the Seventh Infantry Division (Army)
the First Marine Division broke through the North Korean
defenses and united with the advancing parties of the
Eighth Army as it was finally breaking free of Pusan.

Included are materials which deal with Operation
Chromite: with its conception, its planning, the
arguments among military leaders, the logistical
support, the role of the other members of the United
Nations, the landing, the battle for Seoul, and an
evaluation. Official and unofficial reports, documents,
surveys, general histories, and monographs written or
available in English have been utilized.

During World War II historical reporting and
official accounts of battle actions were increased and
systemized.   As a result, American military units
involved in the Korean War were required to keep
official records of their actions. Units from battalion
size up to, and including corps and armies, maintained
records which are now generally available: daily action
reports, unit war diaries, battle narratives,
intelligence information, casualties and logistical
reports. The same types of reports are available for
naval and air actions of the Navy and Marines.

The vast majority of these records are to be found
in the National Archives at one of their specialized
collections. Army records, including the Eighth Army

reports and those of the individual corps and divisions involved can be located at Suitland, Maryland. Marine records can be found at the United States Marine Corps Historical Branch in Washington, DC.

The services have provided their analyses of what happened and have used the Inchon landing as illustrations of both faults to be corrected and successful procedures to be utilized anew.

Materials Excluded

In general this bibliography does not contain "table-top books," division year books, or illustrated collections dealing with weapons, vehicles, or personal equipment of the ranks, unless they pertain directly to the landing. Nor does it include newspaper items and popular journals (except the leading news magazines of the time) nor materials easily found elsewhere. Inasmuch as possible every effort has been made to focus on the landing and the Seoul advance.

Period Covered

Other than general histories, which have been acknowledged for placing the Inchon landing in context, this bibliography focuses on the period from MacArthur's identification of the plan in July 1950, through the fall of Seoul on 28 September 1950. Some materials are included also to provide for overall consideration of the history of the planning and execution of the operation.

ACKNOWLEDGMENTS

The initial collection of these materials began at the Combined Arms Research Library, United States Command and General Staff College, Fort Leavenworth, Kansas. Particular thanks are expressed for the kind consideration and professional help of the staff who not only met our research requests for materials, but also provided an occasional cup of coffee.

It is important also to acknowledge the help of the librarians and staff of several public libraries, particularly those in the Kansas City, Missouri area, who located so many books for this project: Mid-Continent Public Library, Jackson County, Missouri; Benedictine College, Atchison, Kansas; Kansas City, Kansas, Public Library; the Kansas City, Missouri, Public Library, and especially the Trails West Branch of the Kansas City Public Library, located in Independence, Missouri. Thanks also to the fine libraries and librarians at Denver, Colorado; St. Louis, Missouri; Chicago, Illinois; and the New York City Public Library.

Many persons have provided aid and service as a part of their daily routine, and for them, and for those who have gone well "beyond the call of duty," I express my appreciation. To the reference and document librarians at the University of Missouri at Kansas City, to the staff of the Washburn University Library in Topeka, Kansas, to Dr. Tom Peterman at the Park College Library in Parkville, Missouri; Dr. Mary Lou Goodyear,

Associate Director, the Sterling C. Evans Library at Texas A & M University, College Station, Texas; the staff of Baker University Library, Baldwin, Kansas; the librarians at Southwestern Missouri State University in Springfield, Missouri, my gratitude.

Appreciation is given to Dr. Benedict Zobrist and the well trained archivists at the Truman Presidential Library in Independence, Missouri; to Dan Holt and the staff of the Eisenhower Presidential Library and Archives in Abilene, Kansas; to Louise A. Arnold-Friend, reference historian at the United States Army Military History Institute, Carlisle Barracks, Pennsylvania; Lawrence E. Clemens and Barbara Manuel at the Admiral Chester D. Nimitz Library, United States Naval Academy, Annapolis, Maryland; Elena S. Danielson, Associate Archivist, Hoover Institution Archives, Stanford, California; and Joan Phillips of the United States Air University Library, Maxwell Air Force Base, Montgomery, Alabama.

I have been dependent on the collections, and the staff, of the Center for the Study of the Korean War which is located in Independence, Missouri. My appreciation to Joni Wilson, Executive Secretary of the Center for her careful consideration, manuscript development, and final readings which helped me avoid as many errors as possible. This Center, which concentrates on the private papers of Korean veterans, is becoming increasingly valuable to scholars.

Many individuals have been of great help in the on-going search for selected volumes. Among these I must mention Frank Kelley, Roger Revell, Jerry Gilchrist, Tom Peterman, Roger Launius, and Ardis Glenn of Glenn Books.

Editorial appreciation to Professor Myron J. Smith, Jr., the Series Adviser who has been most helpful, and to Mildred Vasan and Emily Okenquist of Greenwood Press who have always been gracious while being efficient.

Paul M. Edwards, Ph.D.
Independence, Missouri

COMMENT ON SOURCES

Since the armistice which halted the costly battles of the Korean War, America has been involved in several other military actions related to the cold war. The attention of the American people was quickly drawn to the growing crisis in Vietnam and, when that was over, to Granada, Panama, Persian Gulf, and to hot spots all over the globe. The Korean War, sandwiched between two important military actions -- the one very popular the other very controversial -- was soon forgotten. For quite some time now the war has defied analysis and resisted historical inquiry. No one has seemed very interested. Few, but the most official of histories, and a series of quick publications for general audiences, have written about the war.

In the intervening years a few excellent and scholarly works have appeared by military historians. Among these are Clay Blair, Roy Appleman, Edwin Hoyt, Walter Karig, Lynn Montross, Nicholas Canzona, Robert Futrell, James Field, Bevin Alexander, Donald Knox, Robert Leckie, James Schnabel, James Stokesbury, Malcolm Cagle, and Frank Manson. But to a large degree what little was produced has been "official" history.

Within the past few years, however, a limited interest in the war has emerged. With the coming of the fiftieth anniversary of World War II some are beginning to remember the war that followed. A few new monographs, articles, and even some books have appeared.

Fresh, with previously unused and unavailable materials, these newer works are the beginning of a historical inquiry that has been lacking for so many years.

However, vast areas of the war have remained unreported, tales unrecounted, and evaluations unmade. Greenwood Press is to be congratulated for acknowledging the importance of this forgotten war and the publication of bibliographies on selected topics. Certainly, of those areas covered, the amphibious landing at Inchon and the associated Seoul campaign has been one of the most interesting. Several excellent works on this campaign have been completed by both American and British authors.

The problem facing the scholar who wants to understand, or write about, the Korean War is not the lack of resources. Documentation is available for most of the war. The problem is in locating it since collections are greatly scattered.

The National Archives is the depository for primary documents on the Korean War; the Modern Military History Headquarters Branch, and the Legislative and Diplomatic Branch of the National Archives, both located in Washington DC, house related documents. Military records are also located at the Modern Military History field Branch at Suitland, Maryland.

The Joint Chiefs of Staff played a significant role in the decision about Inchon. Their messages to and from the General Headquarters in Tokyo are available in published form in <u>Foreign Relations of the United States</u>, Volume 8, 1951, parts 1 and 2. Those which are not published are generally to be located in the Modern Military Records Branch of the National Archives in Washington DC.

Official (staff) historians were at work at almost every level, and the compilations of this staff work is housed at the Army's Center of Military History in Washington DC. Some of the best reports of army units are available in the official publication by Russell A. Gugeler, <u>Combat Action in Korea</u>.

Oral histories of military commanders of those units which participated in the Inchon landing, or the Seoul campaign, are generally available in one of the following: Harry Truman Presidential Library at

Independence, Missouri; the United States Marine Corps History (Division) and Museum, Washington Navy Yard, Washington DC; Mitchell Memorial Library, Special Collection Department, Mississippi State University, Mississippi State, Mississippi; and the MacArthur Memorial Archives in Norfolk, Virginia.

The naval aspects of the war are generally located at the Naval Historical Center, Office of Navy History, Washington DC. For official Marine documentation see the Historical Section, G-3, Headquarters, United States Marine Corps, Navy Yard, Washington, DC.

The scholar who is interested in daily reporting of the war, and related contemporary details should consult complete files of the New York Times, New York Herald-Tribune and the Washington Post.

Some archival limitations should be noted. Although many of the Joint Chief of Staff papers and releases are available in printed form, the records of the internal workings of the Joint Chiefs of Staff are unavailable except to official historians. The same is true of the Douglas MacArthur Papers in Norfolk, Virginia. While the MacArthur collection is an excellent source, there remains a good deal of material still unavailable.

The personal papers of Admiral Forrest P. Sherman are still not available and, as far as can be determined at this time, the dispatches of the Navy high command during the Inchon period, called "Blue Flag Messages," have never been released.

The Korean War was much photographed, and this is especially true of the Inchon period. The largest and best collections are located at the Still Picture Division, Main Archives, or the Anacostia Naval Station, Still Photographic Depository, Washington DC.

Almost every secondary effort which deals with either President Harry Truman and/or General of the Army Douglas MacArthur include some mention of the Korean War, and in that context, of the landing at Inchon. No attempt has been made in this bibliography to list the entirety of these works. Harry Truman apparently did not see the landing as of ultimate significance, and his biographers tend to mention it only in passing.

Books written about General MacArthur are,

generally, efforts to show the General in the best possible light. They have little to say about Korea, and even less about Inchon. When Inchon is mentioned, it tends to be in evidence of the General's accomplishments. These works have not been listed as they do not seem to add anything to a study of the landing. In those cases where works on MacArthur deal directly with the Inchon effort, they are included in this bibliography.

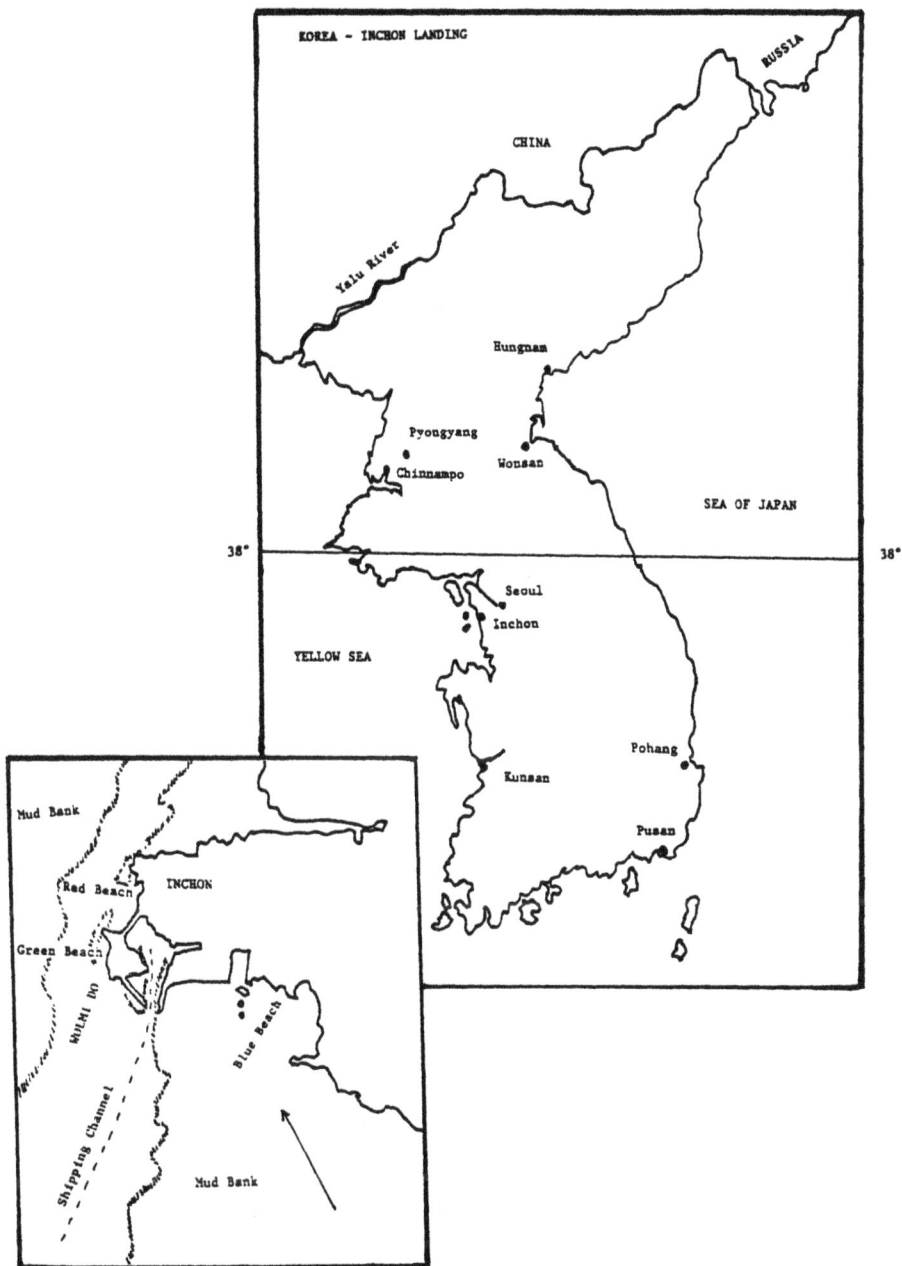

KOREA - INCHON LANDING

CHINA

RUSSIA

Yalu River

Hungnam

Pyongyang

Chinnampo

Wonsan

SEA OF JAPAN

38°   38°

Seoul

Inchon

YELLOW SEA

Pohang

Kunsan

Pusan

Mud Bank

Red Beach   INCHON

Green Beach

WOLMI DO

Blue Beach

Shipping Channel

Mud Bank

Map of the Inchon Landing, Korea, 1950

BRIEF HISTORY
OF THE INCHON LANDING

Celebrations of Independence Day were disregarded as a hastily called conference met at General MacArthur's headquarters on 4 July 1950. During the meetings the General revealed his plan for a counterstroke to be delivered on the west coast of Korea, either at Kunsan or Inchon. He anticipated landing the First Cavalry Division on the beaches, cutting across the North Korean supply lines, recapturing Seoul, and destroying the communication lines so necessary to North Korean military movement. He called the plan Operation Bluehearts, and he wanted it to happen on 22 July 1950, just eighteen days away.

This amphibious action, to be planned and executed in so short a time, was to prove impossible even for MacArthur. The primary difficulty being the lack of troops. Every military unit available to him was desperately needed for the defense of Pusan. And while reinforcements, including the First Provisional Marine Brigade (5th Regiment, 1st Division) were on their way to support Lt. General Walton Walker at Pusan, there simply were not enough troops, supplies, landing craft, or aircraft to accomplish the Inchon mission.

But this was not the end of it. As far as General Douglas MacArthur was concerned such a bold move was essential to turn the tide in Korea. Much of the general's status as a military genius during World War II rested on his use of the amphibious thrust. "Hitting them where they ain't" was not exactly accurate, but he did perfect the job of hitting the Japanese in an island hopping campaign which continually cut their lines of supply and reenforcement.

What MacArthur needed for carrying out his idea of an end-run landing was the First Marine Division. To get the Marines it would be necessary to undertake a major mobilization, including the call-up of the reserves. It was this, as well as numerous arguments over strategy and location, that set in motion a major argument between MacArthur and the Joint Chiefs of Staff -- a dispute between a powerful local commander (who, as a five-star general out-ranked each member of the JCS) and those men charged with leading the military forces of the United States all over the world.

The obvious success of the Inchon landing did a lot to discount those who had argued against it and allowed MacArthur to emerge carrying the disastrous burden that the general could do no wrong. Since then, many have joined the argument over the validity of the plan.

For many the gamble was just too large, the proposed location too desperate, the withdrawal of troops from the Pusan Perimeter defense too extreme. To say that the General received less than total support belies the intensity of the disagreement. These were not just interservice rivalries, nor even political maneuvering, this argument was between serious military commanders over the nature of military engagement.

In retrospect, military historian Bevin Alexander suggests the MacArthur plan was precisely the policy carried out by Hannibal in his victory at Lake Trasimene in 217 BC (p. 151). While MacArthur himself was more likely to relate it to the successful landing of General Wolfe at Quebec.

Inchon had just about every physical difficulty that an amphibious planner could envision. First, amphibious landings usually envision a beach like those faced in the Pacific island landings of World War II. This was not the case at Inchon. The majority of the Inchon coast was broken with small fjords and jutting strips of land. The seaward facing at Inchon was protected by a seawall ranging in height from twelve to fifteen feet. An attacking army would need to scale the walls.

Overlooking the coast were rises of land, the forward slopes of which would be of great advantage to the defenders.

A second major difficulty were the tides which, most of the year, could vary some 32 feet. The draft of landing craft was so deep that only on select days was the tide deep enough to carry them to shore. In 1950 only the 15th and 27th of September were acceptable, and even then there would be no more than two hours of high tide.

A further difficulty was the island of Wolmi-do which sat in the harbor. The island itself was a formidable barrier, and its location prevented a clear run at the harbor. The island was linked to the mainland by a narrow causeway.

Two other, perhaps wider, concerns were raised. The first was the belief that the Eighth Army would not be able to break free and join forces with X Corps in time to accomplish the cut-off of North Korean forces. The second had to do with the larger military situation, for if MacArthur got what he wanted it would mean that the United States would have only the 82nd Airborne Division in reserve; no other combat-ready divisions were available to meet a military challenge anywhere else in the world.

The arguments in favor were few, but in MacArthur's hands they could prove powerful. The most powerful was the simply audacity of it all. No commander would believe such an attempt was being made, and thus no defense could be expected.

Second, the military advantages were overwhelming. Of major importance was the fact that supply routes -- particularly by rail -- of the North Korean forces effectively ran through and near Seoul and that capture would isolate the forces at the Perimeter. The invasion, MacArthur felt, would save 100,000 lives.

Politically, of course, an early landing and success would enable the South Koreans to secure the much needed rice crop which was nearing harvest.

The Joint Chiefs of Staff were most certainly not in full agreement, but they gave final approval on the 8th of September, 1950. Fortunately for the Joint Chiefs President Truman made the final decision.

General Matthew B. Ridgway, who was later to command Eighth Army and eventually to replace MacArthur, was sent to Tokyo to discuss with MacArthur his disagreement with the plan. He admitted that he was won over by the General's wit and charm.

The detailed planning went on under the Inter-Services' Joint Strategic Plans and Operations Group of Far East Command. Eventually Major General Edward M. Almond, MacArthur's Chief of Staff, was appointed to command X Corps which was organized for the landing. The choice was questionable, particularly to the marines who formed the landing force, and this added to the controversy.

The force collected for the landing was formidable. The First Marine Division, under the command of Major General Oliver Smith, selected as its commanders Lt. Colonel Raymond L. Murray for the 5th Regiment, Colonel Lewis B. "Chesty" Puller the 1st Regiment. The 7th Regiment, still enroute, would not arrive in time for the landing. Major General David G. Barr was the commander of the 7th Division (Army).

The 7th Division had been in occupation duty in Japan and was in bad shape. When the war broke out, the "Hourglass Division" had been used to provide replacements for units fighting in Korea. When identified for use at Inchon, the 7th was short more than 400 officers and 8000 enlisted men.

Despite the desperate conditions at Pusan the entire replacement tide was redirected toward the 7th. But when this proved inadequate, the KATUSA (Korean Army Troops Augmentation to United States Army) was integrated. In this so-called "buddy system" untrained, semi-civilian, non-English-speaking South Koreans -- many picked up by what amounted to press gangs-- were placed in the division.

Those units assigned to Inchon also included two 155 Howitzer battalions, an amphibious tractor battalion, and an anti-aircraft battalion, as well as an engineer brigade. In reserve, but not under General Almond's command, was the 187th Airborne Regimental Combat Team. The 1st Regiment of the Korean Marine Corps (KMC) was also assigned.

Air support was provided by the Tactical Air

Command, X Corps, under Brigadier General Thomas J. Cushman (USMC) which was composed of the 12th and 33rd Marine Aircraft Group.

Commanding the 7th Fleet was Vice Admiral Arthur D. Struble with overall command of the collection and arrival of the fleet. Rear Admiral James H. Doyle had naval responsibility for the landing. The collection of 260 vessels, from Australia, Canada, France, Great Britain, Holland, New Zealand and the United States, carried nearly 70,000 men. Of questionable legitimacy (because of the Japanese constitution) were the 37 landing craft (LST) manned by Japanese security forces.

The land forces consisted of the 1st Marine Division, organizationally composed of the 1st, 5th and 7th Regiments. The 5th (1st Provisional Marine Brigade) had been fighting with General Walker at Pusan and was pulled off just in time to regroup and embark. The 1st Regimental Combat Team was being filled from marines on duty with the Atlantic Fleet Marine Force and from the Marine Security Force in the United States.

The division's third regiment, the 7th Regimental Combat Team was a hodge-podge of marines collected from the cadre of the Atlantic Fleet Marine Force, Marine reservists who were volunteering or being called up, and a battalion from Crete. Despite the effort, the 7th Marines did not arrive at Inchon in time for the landing. They were available, however, for the attack on Seoul.

One might well begin the story of the actual landing with the reconnaissance work of Lt. Hi Jong Lee of the Korean Marine Corps who, on 19 August, landed at Inchon to provide a careful analysis of the area considered for attack.

Three weeks later, on the 1st of September Lt. Eugene Clark, USN, led a small unit who also landed at Inchon to carry out last minute reconnaissance. The results of his survey were radioed to the USS Mount McKinley, the command ship, and adjustments were made.

There is little reason to believe that all this was a secret to the North Koreans. In fact some correspondents began calling the proposed landing "Operation Common Knowledge." Yet there appeared to have been some confusion about the location. Inchon, for reasons we have noted, was not likely to have been considered the prime target.   To add to the enemy's confusion several deception ploys were used.

These diversions were not so much to disguise what was happening as to avoid pinpointing the attack any earlier than necessary. One such diversion, carried out ten days before the attack, was the job of Rear Admiral W. Andrewes of the Royal Navy, as his ships approached Wolmi-do from the north and shelled the island.

A second diversion was carried out by United States Special operations from the Royal Navy ship HMS Whitesand Bay at Kunsan, the more probable focus of the attack.   Later, following the attack, the same unit assaulted Kimpo.

On September 5th, ten days prior to the invasion, Naval forces, the Air Force, and Marine air units began the process of softening up the target areas. Corsairs burned the island with napalm, destroying most of the structures and all of the vegetation. Cruisers and destroyers moved into the Flying Fish Channel to aid in the process. On D-Day minus one the waiting cruisers opened fire at what were designated as Blue and Red beaches.

The plan for D-Day consisted of three assault forces assigned to designated attack areas: Blue Beach across the mud flats just south of Inchon; Red Beach north of the causeway and heading into the industrial district of Inchon; and Green Beach which was the defensive island of Wolmi-do that was connected to the mainland by a narrow causeway.

The Green Beach landing began at 0254 with the naval bombardment and at 0600 the landing forces took to their boats.   At 0633, just three minutes late of schedule, the 3rd battalion of the 5th Marines under Lt. Colonel Taplett landed on Wolmi-do.   After encountering light opposition Lt. Colonel Taplett reported by 0800 that Radio Hill was occupied.   Further fighting and an attack using napalm was necessary, but by 1048 hours the causeway was occupied, and just a bit after noon (1215) Green Beach was in full United Nations control.

The unoccupied units of the 5th marines went ashore at Red Beach at the seawalls which would lead them to the heart of the city.   Their goals were to secure

Observatory Hill, more than a thousand yards inland, and
Cemetery Hill on which gun emplacements could look down
on the landing area.

At the same time as the Red Beach assault, the 1st
Marines hit Blue Beach, a mud-flat area near the edge of
the city. They also had a seawall to contend with.

By the morning of the next day the beaches were
linked and the marines advanced inland. By the end of
the day Inchon was under marine control. The first
phase of the operation was over and was successful.
Inchon had been taken with fewer than 200 casualties,
only 20 fatal. One naval officer was killed by return
fire during the bombardment.

Ahead was Kimpo airfield which was taken almost
immediately as the marines headed for the Han River.
The 187th Airborne Regimental Combat Team filed into
Kimpo and joined the marines left flank. The Korean
Marines supported the flanks as well.

On the 18th of September the 7th Infantry Division
(Army) was ashore south of Inchon and moving, parallel
to the marines, toward Seoul.

The plan that MacArthur had envisioned was that
of an anvil and hammer. The Inchon landing and movement
across the Han was to serve as the anvil while Walker
and the Eighth Army was the hammer. By the 16th of
September more than 150,000 United Nations troops were
involved. The 2nd, 24th, and 25th Infantry as well as
the 1st Cavalry were organized into I Corps. IX Corps
would soon be in place. With F-51's from the Air Force
strafing and napalming, the retreating North Korean
forces were eventually pushed out of Pohang-dong.

From the 16th to the end of September the fight
moved northeast. Then, near midnight on the 26th the
advanced forces of X Corps and Walker's Eighth Army met.
MacArthur, aware of the political implications of a
triumphal entry, returned Seoul to President Rhee on the
29th of September, 1950. It had been just a little over
three months since the war began, and fourteen days
after the landing at Inchon.

CHRONOLOGY OF
SIGNIFICANT EVENTS

1950:

25 June   North Korean People's Army (NKPA), crosses
               38th parallel and invades the Republic of
               Korea (South Korea).

27 June   President Truman authorizes the use of
               United States ground troops.

5 July   First forces (Task Force Smith) land.

7 July   United Nations authorize military support
               for South Korea with a unified command
               under an American general.

23 July   General Douglas MacArthur plans amphibious
               landing mid-September (Operation Chromite)
               but does not name Inchon as the target.

12 August   MacArthur names Inchon as invasion site.

15 August   Special Planning Staff established, nucleus
               for X Corps developed as separate command.

19 August   ROK Marines land at Tong Yong for Inchon
               rehearsals. Lt. Lee (Korean Marine Corps)
               lands at Inchon for reconnaissance.

23 August

MacArthur holds Tokyo conference with Joint Chiefs of Staff to argue plan for Inchon.

26 August

MacArthur establishes X Corps for the Inchon landing with his Chief of Staff, General Almond, in command.

1 September

Lt. Eugene Clark, USN, begins two week reconnaissance (Operation Trudy Jackson).

3 September

Typhoon Jane hits Kobe, Japan. 1st Marine Division departs for Inchon.

5 September

Ships of the Royal Navy shell Wolmi-do from the northern approach as part of a deception plan.

6 September

Lt. Colonel Murray's 5th Marine Regiment withdrawn from the Pusan Perimeter for embarkation to Inchon.

10-12 September

Colonel Chesty Puller's 1st Marine Regiment sails from Kobe. Lt. Colonel Murray's 5th Marine Regiment sails from Pusan. General Barr's 7th (Army) Infantry Division sails from Yokohama.

13 September

Typhoon Kezia hits. MacArthur and his staff depart on USS Mount McKinley. HMS Whitesand Bay attacks Kunsan in deception ploys. Naval bombardment begins. Rear Admiral Higgins with four cruisers and six destroyers move up Flying Fish Channel to bombard Inchon and Wolmi-do.

15 September

Maj. General Smith, First Marine Division, takes operational command at Inchon. Lt. Colonel Taplett's 3rd

Battalion, 5th Marines land Wolmi-do. Lt Colonel Murray's 5th Marines land on Red Beach.   Colonel Puller 1st Marines land on Blue Beach.

17 September	5th Marines take Ascom City. MacArthur comes ashore at Inchon. Admiral Struble's 7th Fleet flagship <u>USS Rochester</u> shoots down YAK plane in Inchon harbor.
18 September	5th Marines take and secure Kimpo Airfield. Maj General Barr's 7th (Army) Division [32nd Infantry] ashore at Inchon.
19 September	<u>USS Missouri</u> arrives near Inchon. Remainder of the 7th (Army) Division ashore.
20 September	5th Marines cross Han River, north and west of Seoul.
21 September	Maj. Gen. Almond assumes command of X Corps ashore. Colonel Puller's 1st Marines take Yong Dong. 7th Marine Regiment unloads at Inchon. Lt. Van Sant's tank platoon enters Suwon.
24 September	Colonel Puller's 1st Marines cross Han and enter Seoul.
25 September	Army's 32nd Infantry Regiment crosses Han and takes South Mountain.
26 September	First tenuous link-up between advance troops of X Corps and Eighth Army.
27 September	Government House (Seoul) is taken by the marines.
28 September	25,000 enemy defenders flee Seoul as the city falls.

29 September   MacArthur returns South Korea to
                      President Rhee. UN forces halt at
                      38th Parallel.

30 September   Operation Chromite declared a
                      success.

ARCHIVES AND DOCUMENTS

ARCHIVAL MATERIALS

Combined Arms Research Library, United States Command
and General Staff College (Fort Leavenworth, Kansas)
    USAF Airborne Operations, World War II and Korean
    War [Official use only].

Defense Audiovisual Agencies, Still Photographic
Depository, No. 168 (Anacostia Naval Station,
Washington, DC)
    Still photography: Korean War period.

Federal Records Center (Kansas City, Missouri)
    KMAG: A General File, 1949-1950.

Harry S Truman Presidential Library (Independence,
Missouri)
    Korean War: General File.
    Korean War: Department of Defense.
    Papers:
        Dean Acheson
        Eben Ayers NUCMC 76-97
        David E. Bell NUCMC 76-1691
        George M. Elsey NUCMC 77-901

John F. Melby NUCMC 1713
John H. Muccio - Interview
Frank Pace NUCMC 65-131
John Summers NUCMC 75-602
Harry S Truman NUCMC 65-145, 77-910
Harry Vaughan NUCMC 65-144

Hoover Institution on War, Stanford University
(Stanford, California)
Miscellaneous File, Korea,
Accession TS Korea U58.
North Korean propaganda materials.

Library of Congress (Washington, DC)
Foreign Broadcast Information Service Daily
Reports on microfilm. These include daily
translations of Chinese, North Korean, and
Russian radio broadcasts and news releases
for the period of the Inchon invasion.

MacArthur Memorial Bureau of Archives (Norfolk, Virginia)
Allied Translator and Interpreter Section,
Interrogation Reports.
Messages between MacArthur and the Joint Chiefs
General Headquarters, United Nations
Command, 1945-1951, United States Air Force
in Korea.
Messages Joint Chief of Staff, Record Group 9.
VIP File, Record Group 10.

Modern Military Records Branch, National Archives
(Washington, DC)
Army Plans and Operations Division,
Record Group 319.
Department of the Army, Record Group 336.
G. C. Stewart "My Service During the Korea War."
Intelligence (G-2) Library, United States Army,
Record Group 319.

Intelligence Summaries, North Korean, Record
     Group 739.
James H. Dill "Diary and Personal Adventures."
Messages between the Joint Chiefs of Staff and
     General Headquarters in Tokyo, Record
     Group 218. Most of these are published in
     Foreign Relations of the United States,
     volume 7, 1951.
Military History Section of Headquarters, Far East
     Command, "History of the Korean War,
     Chronology, 25 June 1950 - 31 December
     1951."
National Security Council, Office of the
     Secretary of Defense, Record Group
     330.
"Record of Actions Taken by the Joint Chiefs of
     Staff Relative to the United Nations
     Operations in Korea from 25 June 1950 to
     11 April 1951, Prepared by Them,"
     107 pages.
Roy Appleman's collection of letters and
     comments from participants in the Korean
     War.
7th Division, Unit History.

The National Archives, Federal Records Center (Suitland,
Maryland)
     Captured Enemy Documents "Far East Command,
          Enemy Documents: Korean Operations" Allied
          Translator and Interpreter Section.
     Far East Command GHQ Support and Participation
          in the Korean War, Notes and Manuscript by
          Lt. Colonel J. F. Schnabel.
     Far Eastern Command, Record Group 332.
     Files relating to Roy Appleman South to the
          Naktong, North to the Yalu and Lynn
          Montross and Nicholas Canzona The Pusan
          Perimeter as official publications.
     1st Provisional Brigade, United States Marine
          Corps, are housed at Suitland but remain
          under the control of the Historical Branch
          USMC.

Historical Reports, United States Military
Advisors Group to the Republic of Korea
(KMAG) 1949-1950.
S. L. A. Marshall interview of "Chesty" Puller,
unpublished.
Supreme Commander for the Allied Powers, Record
Group 331.
War Diaries (to 1 December 1950) Record Group
407.

National Personnel Records Center, Military Personnel
Records (St. Louis, Missouri)
Military personnel (201) files.

Naval Historical Center, Office of Navy History
(Washington, DC)
Chief of Naval Operations File.
Command Carrier Division I "Report of Task Force
77, Operations During the Korean Campaign
(June 1950 - January 1951).
ComNavFE "Command and Historical Reports
(September - November 1950) 1954.
ComPhibGru I. "Report of Operations (June 1950 -
January 1951)."
General Headquarters, Tokyo, History of the
North Korean Army.
Hq X Corps Operation Chromite War Diary Summary,
August 15 - September 30, 1950.
PacFlt: Interim Evaluation Reports. Number 1
(25 June - 15 November 1950) 1951.
Personal Papers:
Admiral C. T. Joy
Admiral R. A. Ofstie
Report of Proceedings (September 1950 -
November 1951).
Sailing Directions, Southeast Coast of Siberia
and Korea, 1951.
7th Fleet Action Reports.
Ship to Shore Movement, USN Office of Naval
History.

War Diary, Republic of Korea Navy (Task Force
    96.7/95.7).
Oral Histories
    Arleigh A. Burke
    Jackson S. Parker
    William Sebald
    John S. Thach

Still Picture Division, Main Archives (Washington, DC)
    Still photographs of the Korean War.

United Nations Archives (Washington, DC)
    United Nations Documents, 1946-1960   Readex
    Microprint Edition (Readex, New York: Microprint
    Corporation, 1978).
        Military, as well as diplomatic efforts by
        the United States in the United Nations is
        apparent in these documents which, if used,
        require extensive work in the indexes,
        which are housed separately and on
        microfiche.

United States Army Military History Institute (Carlisle
Barracks, Pennsylvania)
    Oral History Collection
        Edward M. Almond
        Matthew B. Ridgway
        Maxwell D. Taylor
    Personal Notes of General E. M. Almond Covering
        Military Operations in Korea, September
        1950 - July 1951.
    Personal papers:
        Lt. General Edward M. Almond (Commander of
            X Corps)
        Brigadier General S. L. A. Marshall
        Major General Charles Willoughby

United States Marine Corps History (Division) Museum
(Navy Yard, Washington, DC)

"A Brief History of the First Marines"
Intelligence Summary, General Headquarters,
Far East Command, Military Intelligence
Section, General Staff (June 1950 - March
1951).

Battle Reports of the ROK Marine Corps, Seoul,
ROK Seoul, ROK Marine Corps, 1962.

Diary File (Battalions) First Marine Division
1st Marine Division Special Action Reports,
FMF, for the Inchon-Seoul Operation, volume
1. Historical Section, Intelligence Annex,
G-3, Hq USMC.

Marine Corps Board Study, Evaluation of the
Influence of Marine Corps Forces on the
Course of the Korean War, August 4, 1952,
in Marine Corps Historical Branch.

Monograph and Comment File, volume 2. Marine
Operations in Korea, Historical Section,
G-3 Hq USMC.

"Notes on the Operations of the 1st Marine
Division During the First Nine Months of
the Korean War, 1950 - 1951," Manuscript
File.

Oral History Reports
Alpha A. Bowser
Edward A. Craig
Oliver P. Smith
Gerald C. Thomas

Smith, Oliver P. (Major General, USMC)
"Chronicle of the Operations of the 1st
Marine Division during the First Nine
Months of the Korean War, 1950 - 1951,"
Manuscript File.

Smith, Oliver P. unpublished Aide-Memoir,
Korea, 1950-51 in Marine Corps Historical
Branch.

United States Marine Corps Board Study "An
Evaluation of the Influence of Marine Corps
Forces on the Course of the Korean War"
[August 4, 1950 - December 15, 1950] 2
volumes, R & O file.

PUBLISHED DOCUMENTS

Congressional Records

001 Hearings on the Military Situation in the Far East.
Congressional Record, Senate, 82nd Congress, 1st
Session, 1951.
    Voluminous collection of testimony concerning the
military situation, objectives, Inchon landing, and
General MacArthur's release from command.

002 "The Korean War and Related Matters." Report of
the Subcommittee on Internal Security to the Senate
Judiciary Committee, 84th Congress, 1st Session.
Washington: Government Printing Office, 1951.
    Primarily concerned with the MacArthur dismissal,
but considers earlier aspects of his command, and the X
Corps versus Eighth Army command structure.

003 Report of the Subcommittee on Internal Security;
Subcommittee to Investigate the Administration of the
Internal Security Act and Other Internal Security Laws
to the Committee on the Judiciary, Part 25, Senate,
84th Congress, 1st Session, January 21, 1955.
Government Printing Office, 1955.
    Lt. General Edward Almond's testimony explains the
purposes of Inchon and the value of a divided command.

Department of State Publications

BOOKS

004 Department of Defense. Semi-annual Reports of the
Secretary of Defense, and Semi-annual Reports of the
Secretary of the Army, Secretary of the Navy, Secretary
of the Air Force, January 1 to June 30 and July 1 to
December 30, 1950. Washington, DC: Government Printing
Office, 1950-1955.
    These reports on military action are filed by field
and theater commanders, then to service secretaries, and
include Inchon.

005   Department of State Publication. <u>United States</u>
<u>Policy in the Korean Conflict, July 1950 - February</u>
<u>1951</u>. Washington, DC: Government Printing Office, 1954.
     Considers the political and policy aspect of the
American   involvement   in   Korea   and   the   policy
considerations behind several of the military actions,
including Inchon.

006   <u>Records of the Joint Chiefs of Staff: Part I,</u>
<u>Meetings of the Joint Chiefs of Staff, 1946-1953</u>.
Frederick, Maryland: University Publication, 1980.
     Minutes of the meetings of the Joint Chiefs during
the Korean War, especially useful in considering both
the military view of why the United States was involved,
and how it fought the first period including the
decision concerning Inchon.   Microfilm available in
eight reels.   Declassified in 1970.

007   <u>Records of the Joint Chiefs of Staff: Part II, The</u>
<u>Far East, 1946-1953</u>. Frederick, Maryland: University
Publication, 1980.
     Documents of military activities and policies
during the pre-war Korean involvement, the invasion and
American military reaction, as well as the first year of
defense.   Very helpful in trying to understand the
military mind, the policy of involvement, and how the
war was to be fought.   Microfilm available in fourteen
reels.

Official Documents

BOOKS

008   <u>Foreign Relations of the United States, 1950:</u>
<u>Korea</u>. Washington, DC: Government Printing Office, 1976.
     Contains the policy messages that shot back and
forth to Korea (as well as Russia, Great Britain, and
India) on the political implications of military action.
731 - 799.

009   United States, Aerospace Studies Institute Concept Division. _Guerrilla Warfare and Airpower in Korea 1950-53_. Maxwell Air Force Base, Air University: Aerospace Studies Institute, 1964.
     A brief survey of interdiction in Korea, primarily during the "stalemate" period of the War.

010   United States, Department of the Army, Office of Military History. _Korea, 1950_. Washington, DC: 1952.
     General survey of political entries and military policy relating to the outbreak of fighting and the early response.

011   United States Navy, Pacific Fleet and Pacific Ocean Area.   _CINCPACFLT Interim Evaluation Reports, Korea, 1950-1953_.   Wilmington, Delaware: Scholarly Resources (Microfilm).
     Accompanied by temporary guide, also microfilmed, six reels, 35 mm.

SECONDARY SOURCES

AUTOBIOGRAPHIES, BIOGRAPHIES, AND MEMOIRS

BOOKS

012 Army Times. (editor). The Banners and the Glory: The Story of General Douglas MacArthur. New York: G. P. Putnam's and Sons, 1965. 189 pages, index, illustrations.
   A hazy, publicity directed, account of General Douglas MacArthur, from the time when he was identified as Commander-in-Chief of United Nations forces through the victory at Inchon. This account displays a strong case for the singular role the General played in the "successes" of Korea.

013 Berry, Henry. Hey, Mac, Where Ya Been? New York: St. Martins's Press, 1988. 370 pages, index, illustrations, maps.
   An excellent collection of oral history memories of the United States Marines during the Korean War. These personal accounts are both humorous and deadly. The retelling of the soldier's story gives an excellent picture of the war as it was seen by those fighting it. The assault and landing at Inchon is reviewed in five interviews.

014   Davis, Burke. <u>Marine: The Life of Lt. General Lewis B. (Chesty) Puller, USMC (Ret.)</u>. Boston: Brown, 1962. 403 pages, index, illustrations, maps.
     More than any other man, Lt. General Lewis B. "Chesty" Puller, USMC, was the symbol of the fighting marine. From the command of horse Marines in Peking to the landing at Inchon, Puller was at the center of America's military efforts. Chapters 15 and 16 of this excellent biography deal with Puller's role in the preparation and execution of the Inchon landing.

015   Greenwood, C. I. <u>Once Upon a Time</u>. Springfield, Illinois: Phillips, 1989. 214 pages, illustrations, photos, cartoons.
     This is a privately printed account of the battle action of Marine Gunnery Sergeant C. I. Greenwood who landed with the marines at Inchon. A highly personal, but very informative, account of the "troops" side of the landing. Manages to avoid much analysis and blame.

016   Gunther, John. <u>The Riddle of MacArthur: Japan, Korea and the Far East</u>. New York: Harpers, 1951. 240 pages, index.
     Written far too early to be very informative about Korea or Inchon, and a number of the conclusions he draws are proven wrong by the end of the war. But he does try to explain MacArthur in sort of a folksy account in which he identifies General MacArthur's farsighted understanding of the Inchon situation, his victory at Inchon, and the unkindness of criticism leveled against MacArthur.

017   Higgins, Marguerite. <u>War in Korea: The Report of a Woman Combat Correspondent</u>. Garden City, New York: Doubleday & Company, 1951. 223 pages, illustrations, map.
     A highly critical and overly-dramatic book by Marguerite Higgins, the first of the women correspondents at the front in Korea. She went ashore as a "member in good standing" of the fifth wave of Marines at Inchon. While critical of the Army troops during the first few months, and the "unnecessary" retreat, she gives the marines good press.

018   Higgins, Trumbull.   <u>Korea and the Fall of
MacArthur: A Precis in Limited War</u>.   New York: Oxford
University Press, 1960.   229 pages, index, notes,
bibliography, map.
      An interesting study of the relationship between
civilian and military command during wartime.   The
author concludes   MacArthur was basically a military
genius but he did not understand the political
implications of either his victory at Inchon, or his
push to cross the 38th parallel.

019   Hunt, Frazier.   <u>The Untold Story of Douglas
MacArthur</u>. New York: The Devin-Adair Company, 1954.   533
pages, index, illustrations.
      Hunt was a friend of General MacArthur, and covered
his headquarters for the press on "the war he was not
permitted to win."   This reporter's objectivity is
completely lost, and some facts seem to be lopsided.
But he has interesting "insider" comments about
MacArthur and Inchon, as well as commentary on the
General's success prior to the time Truman pulled his
"crime of the century."   451 - 478.

020 Kenney, George C. <u>The MacArthur I Know</u>.   New York:
Duell, Sloan and Pearce, 1951.   264 pages.
      A "political biography" written by a close
MacArthur associate who uses the occasion to engage in
more than a little hero worship.   He discusses the
Korean connection in broad terms and identifies the
Inchon landing as a stroke of genius and as if it were
the only military action open to them at the time. 207 -
225.

021 Knox, Donald. <u>The Korean War: Pusan to Chosin: An
Oral History</u>. Volume 1. New York: Harcourt, 1985.   697
pages, index, illustrations, maps.
      An oral account of phases of the war, the first
volume of which deals with Pusan to the Yalu.   He
includes several fine and informative accounts from
those who were there during the Inchon campaign.   He
accounts MacArthur's "flamboyance and penchant for grand
gestures" so clearly shown, or so harshly tested.   194-
308.

022 MacArthur, Douglas. <u>Reminiscences</u>. New York:
Da Capo Paperback, 1964. 448 pages, index.
     This is a great disappointment, considering it is
really the only major effort on the part of a world
figure to explain his actions. Part nine of this memoir
deals with the war in Korea but the seeming lack of
interest in the Inchon campaign appears strange. 325 -
350.

023 Maihafer, Harry J. <u>From the Hudson to the Yalu:
West Point '49 in the Korean War</u>. College Station:
Texas A & M University Press, 1993. 279 pages, index,
illustrations, maps.
     A well written personal account which follows the
lives of West Point class of 1949. So many of these
young officers served in Korea, including the campaign
at Inchon. Good account of life in the field at the 2nd
lieutenant level.

024 Manchester, William. <u>American Caesar: Douglas
MacArthur, 1880 - 1964</u>. New York: Dell, 1978.   960
pages, illustrations, maps.
     Manchester is not afraid to expose MacArthur's
warts, nor to express appreciation for his efforts and
abilities. MacArthur was no more or less than his times
and environment demanded. The Korean War was a final
call for an old hero and he took full advantage of it.
According to Manchester, MacArthur gambled everything on
the Inchon landing and won, only to lose it in his
misreading of military and political follow-up. 664 -
750.

025   Marshall, Samuel L. A. and Cate Marshall.
(editor). <u>Bringing Up the Rear: A Memoir</u>.   San
Francisco: Presidio Press, 1979.   310 pages, index,
illustrations, maps.
     Marshall, one of America's most respected military
historians, saw military service for over thirty years
and wrote this history of his role in military affairs.
His comments on Inchon are essential for any broad
understanding. While the comments on Inchon are brief,
it includes opinion and analysis of the landing at
Inchon.

026   McCullough, David. Truman. New York: Simon and
Schuster, 1992. 1116 pages, index, illustrations.
    By far the most readable, if not the most complete
biography of President Truman. While there is nothing
specific on Inchon, President Harry Truman was a full
participant   in   military   and   political   decisions
concerning Korea. This author provides a clearer
understanding of Truman's policies and attitudes and is
essential to fully comprehend and analyze this period of
confusion.

027   Murphy, Edward F. Korean War Heroes. Novato,
California: Presidio Press, 1992. 304 pages, index,
illustrations, maps, bibliography.
    An account of the 131 Medal of Honor winners during
the Korean War. Chapter 3 "Hammer and Anvil" deals with
those awarded during the Inchon landing and the follow-
up attack on Seoul, providing some excellent insights of
life on the line.

028   Parry, Francis F. Three-War Marine: The Pacific *
Korea * Vietnam. Pacifica, California: Pacifica Press,
1987. 272 pages, maps.
    Colonel Parry commanded an artillery battalion in
Korea; at Inchon, Seoul, and later at the Chosin
Reservoir. His account is of taking a "makeshift unit
into combat at the outset of a war for which his nation
was unprepared." (cover). Good on the daily activities
of an artillery unit, and one of the few dealing with
Marine artillery.

029   Sawyer, Robert K. Military Advisors in Korea:
KMAG in Peace and War. Army Historical Series,
Washington DC: Center of Military History, 1962. 216
pages, index, illustrations.
    With the outbreak of the war, and the essential
victory of North Korean forces, members of KMAG soon had
to drop their advisory role and become operational.
This they did rather unsuccessfully. But as the tide
turned, and Republic of Korea troops were involved at
the Inchon campaign, the members of the Korean Military
Advisory Group was there directing, organizing, and
mentoring troops.

030   Schaller, Michael.   <u>Douglas MacArthur: The Far Eastern General</u>.   New York: Oxford University Press, 1989.   320 pages, index, illustrations, maps.
A well considered biography of Douglas MacArthur as general and statesman.   The coverage of the Inchon plan itself is limited (198 - 201) but the look at the General, his agenda, and his expectations all place the Inchon plan in proper perspective.   Under the circumstances, Schaller tells us, one should have expected nothing less than a wide dramatic sweep which would, as it did, refocus the world's attention on MacArthur.

031   Schott, Joseph L.   <u>Above and Beyond</u>.   New York: G.P. Putnam's Sons, 1963.   314 pages, appendix.
One hundred and thirty-one Medals of Honor were awarded during the Korean War.   Chapter 21 of this work deals with medals given as a result of the Inchon-Seoul campaign.   There are several accounts of the men and their activities leading to the heroism during this campaign.

032   Sebald, William J. and Russell Brines.   <u>With MacArthur in Japan: A Personal History of the Occupation</u>.   New York: W. W. Norton & Company, Inc., 1965.   318 pages, illustrations.
This is primarily an account of the highly successful occupation of Japan, and MacArthur's role as the Allied representative.   The Korean War is a minor part of this work, but the discussion of the relationship between the Inchon landing and General MacArthur's foreign policy is explained in detail and well done.   177 - 210.

033   Smith, Robert.   <u>MacArthur in Korea: The Naked Emperor</u>.   New York: Simon and Schuster, 1982.   256 pages, index, illustrations, bibliography.
Designed as a tribute to Douglas MacArthur it nevertheless deals openly with the leader's limitations, primarily his arrogance and recklessness.   Inchon is an example of both of these conditions.   Smith does not make his case very effectively.   Indexed throughout but heavy 70 - 77, 151 - 153.

034 Spanier, John W. The Truman-MacArthur Controversy
and The Korean War. New York: W. W. Norton & Company,
Inc. 1965. 311 pages, index.
     The success at Inchon reaffirmed MacArthur's
conviction that it was wise to follow the bold course
whenever the military situation appeared bleak. Inchon,
based on the concept of the Wolfe campaign against
Quebec (at least according to the press), was the clear-
cut difference between the "will to win" and
"vacillation." Despite General Omar N. Bradley's
feelings to the contrary, MacArthur proved that
amphibious warfare and its success was not a thing of
the past.

035 Steinberg, Alfred. Douglas MacArthur. New York:
G. P. Putnam's Sons, 1961. 192 pages, index, maps.
     A typical short account of the life of the highly
controversial general, Douglas MacArthur. What is
surprising is the seemingly insignificant role of Korea
in this account, and the lack of any real understanding
of the Korean War, and of the landing at Inchon. 169 -
171.

036 Tomedi, Rudy. No Bugles, No Drum: An Oral History
of the Korean War. New York: John Wiley and Sons, 1993.
259 pages, index, illustrations.
     An oral history of the Korean War, following the
war as it was seen by individuals. The areas are well
distributed, one section (29 - 39) dealing with the
Inchon landing, and the larger battle (Operation
Chromite) in order. To many, Inchon, was nothing
spectacular.

037 Truman, Harry S. Memoirs: Years of Trial and Hope.
Volume 2. Garden City, New York: Doubleday & Company,
1956. 594 pages, index.
     President Truman was in the middle of the conflict
both in and about Korea. As Commander-in-Chief his
approval was necessary for any policy change and it was
the President who gave final authority for the Inchon
landing. He says surprisingly little about the why of
his decision, but his early involvement is well
documented, and indexed.

038 Whitney, Courtney. <u>MacArthur: His Rendezvous with History</u>. New York: Alfred A. Knopf, 1956. 547 pages, index.

A strong biography of MacArthur as military commander. The author supports MacArthur in the "great debate" over the Inchon landing, though he provides little defense other than MacArthur's wisdom, military knowledge, and a general ability. 342 - 357.

039   Willoughby, Charles A. and John Chamberlain. <u>MacArthur 1941-1951</u>.   New York: McGraw-Hill Book Company, Inc. 441 pages, index, illustrations, maps.

A good account of MacArthur, but the Korea period lacks the analysis that would be possible twenty years later. The Inchon landing is seen as just one more in a long line of successful amphibious victories for the general. 366 - 378.

ARTICLES

040 Ickes, Harold L. "MacArthur Is Always Right" <u>New Republic</u> 124:11 (March 12, 1951) 16.

Ickes reminds us that MacArthur's ability to turn defeat into victory lies is in his use of words, not troops.   Questions his association with Nationalist China.

041 Martin, Harold H. "Toughest Marine in the Corps" <u>Saturday Evening Post</u> 224:38 (March 22, 1952) 40 - 41, 105 - 110.

Another account of the infamous Lewis B. "Chesty" Puller who was commander of a marine unit which landed at Inchon. In recounting his "beer versus ice cream" story it tells us more about Puller's unorthodox behavior and views than it does the events in Korea. Inchon is considered.

042 Parrott, L. "And Now MacArthur of Korea" <u>New York Times Magazine</u> (August 20, 1950) 50 - 51.

A high profile "public relations" type effort which identifies MacArthur, then 70, as a powerful and hardworking leader who may well be the salvation of the United States in Asia.

043 Timmons, Bascom M. "MacArthur's Greatest Battle" Collier's 125:25 (December 16, 1950) 13 - 15, 65 - 66.
This is a better than average account of MacArthur's background and the suggestion that the General's classic inception of amphibious warfare was the turning point of the war. "One of the most decisive strategic operations of all times." Timmons writes a convincing article on the support of the "only action possible" thesis.

BIBLIOGRAPHIES, DICTIONARIES, AND REFERENCES

BOOKS

044   The Army Almanac.   Harrisburg: The Stackpole Company, 1959.   797 pages, name and topic indexes.
Contains the table of organization and management for the United States Army. The army underwent a basic reorganization in 1949, which was tested in the early days of the Korean War.

045   Association of Asian Studies.   Cumulative Bibliography of Asian Studies 1941-1965: Subject Bibliography. Four volumes. Boston: Hall Publishing, 1970-1972.
Volumes three and four of this carefully collected bibliography contain numerous articles dealing with the Korean War. The lack of an index makes it difficult to use. All works listed are available in English.

046   Bibliography of Social Science Periodicals and Monograph Series Republic of Korea, 1945-1961. Washington, DC: Superintendent of Documents, Government Printing Office, 1962. Foreign Bibliography Series, P-92, number 9, iv-48.
A selected bibliography of articles and monographs dealing with Korea covering the period from the American occupation through the war. Some deal with Inchon. All listed are available in English.

047 Blanchard, Carroll H. Jr. <u>Korean War Bibliography and Maps of Korea</u>. Albany, New York: Korean Conflict Research Foundation, 1964. 181 pages, maps, subject and author index.
     The early phase of a program to collect and identify materials dealing with the War. His subject arrangements are somewhat difficult and by now the work is extremely dated.

048 Burns, Richard D. <u>Harry S. Truman: A Bibliography of His Times and Presidency</u>. Wilmington, Delaware: Scholarly Resources, Inc., 1984. 297 pages, index, illustrations.
     Chapter 8 deals with the pre-war concerns, including the American occupation of Korea (1945-1950). Chapter 10 deals with President Truman and the war, and includes materials identified under the heading "Inchon-Seoul."

049 Chung, Yong Sun. (compiler). <u>Korean: A Selected Bibliography, 1959-1963</u>. Kalamazoo, Michigan: Korean Research and Publications, 1965.
     The title is confusing. These are works about the war (1950 - 1953) which became available in the period 1959 - 1963. These materials include some North Korean and Chinese sources, most of which are available in English, though very hard to locate.

050   Coletta, Paolo E. (compiler). <u>A Selected Bibliography of American Naval History</u>. Lanham, New York: University Press of America, 1988 (revised).
     This massive listing of works on naval history includes not only articles, books, and monographs but theses and dissertations as well. More than a hundred works are on the Korean War, a few which relate to the Inchon landing.

051 Dollen, Charles. <u>Bibliography of the United States Marine Corps</u>. New York: The Scarecrow Press, Inc., 1963. 115 pages.
     Well identified collection of books and articles relating to the Marine Corps. A good index makes it especially useful. Dated but still helpful.

052   Greenwood, John. (compiler). <u>American Defense</u>
<u>Policy Since 1945: A Preliminary Bibliography</u>.
Lawrence, Kansas: University Press of Kansas, 1973.
    Lists more than sixty works on the outbreak and
early political considerations of the Korean War,
including the Inchon decision and the crossing of the
38th parallel. A good solid collection greatly limited
by the lack of an index.

053   Hyatt, Joan. (compiler). <u>Korean War, 1950-1953:</u>
<u>Selected References</u>.   Maxwell Air Force Base, Air
University Library, 1990. 63 pages, no index.
    A small but very valuable collection of Korean War
materials collected by a bibliographic expert on the
war, and available at the Air University Library.

054   Imperial War Museum Library. <u>The War in Korea,</u>
<u>1950-1953, A List of Selected References</u>. London: War
Museum Library, 1961.
    This mimeographed list produced by the Imperial War
Museum (Library) staff contains more than 350 books,
articles, and monographs in English on Commonwealth
forces who served in the Korean War. It also includes
references to American units, but is dated.

055   <u>Key Korean War Battles Fought in the Republic of</u>
<u>Korea</u>. APO, San Francisco: Headquarters, Eighth United
States Army, 1972.
    A short, one sided, and limited account of the
significant battles fought by United States Eighth Army
and X Corps during the Korean War. Primarily a
bibliographic source of materials which are available to
the researcher. Hard to acquaint title with contents.

056   <u>Korean Conflict: A Collection of Historical</u>
<u>Manuscripts on the Korean Campaign Held by the U. S.</u>
<u>Army Center of Military History</u>.   Washington, DC:
Library of Congress, Photoduplication Services, 1975.
9 reels (Unclassified microfilm).
    A history (both subject and date) of material
available at the Army Center of Military History. Many
of these are only peripherally related, but all in all
a useful compilation.

057 Leckie, Robert. <u>Great American Battles</u>. New York:
Random House, 1968.   177 pages, index, illustrations.
     A collection of accounts of major American battles
which includes the Inchon-Seoul campaign.   Leckie, a
well known military historian, tries to explain <u>how</u>
Americans fought.   There is little new information here
but contains an interesting account of how MacArthur won
over the Joint Chiefs of Staff to support the Inchon
landing.

058 Matray, James I. (editor). <u>Historical Dictionary of
the Korean War</u>. Westport, Connecticut: Greenwood Press,
1991.   648   pages,   index,   illustrations,   maps,
bibliography.
     Provides a useful tool to assist in understanding
the Korean War, describes significant persons involved,
controversies,   military   operations,   and   policy.
Accurate and well constructed, this dictionary is
excellent for the occasional reference to operations,
persons, and locations.

059 McFarland, Keith D.   <u>The Korean War: An Annotated
Bibliography</u>. New York: Garland Publishers, 1986. 461
pages, subject and author index.
     An excellent collection of annotated materials
dealing with the war.   It is well arranged and easy to
identify, cross referenced in index.   The annotations
are brief but crisp.   In his citation he does not
identify indexes in individual works. The bibliography
includes a section on the Inchon landing.   Other than
the fact so many new materials have appeared since 1986,
this continues to be an excellent and scholarly research
aid.

060   O'Quinlivan, Michael and James S. Santelli.   <u>An
Annotated Bibliography of the United States Marines in
the Korean War</u>. Washington, DC: Historical Branch G-3
Division, Headquarters US Marines, 1962.   Revised
edition 1970.
     A good, but dated, listing of materials dealing
with the United States Marine Corps action during the
Korean War.   Annotations very limited.   Needs to be
revised since so much new material is now available.

061   Park, Hong-Kyu. The Korean War: An Annotated Bibliography. Marshall, Texas: Demmer Co., Inc., 1971. 29 pages.

A brief and very selective work which concentrates on Korean entries (in English) without special identification. This is very valuable as one of the sources of Korean entries but the material is limited and dated.

062   Schuon, Karl. U.S. Marine Corps Biographical Dictionary.   New York: Watts, 1963. 278 pages, illustrations.

Selects brief sketches of officers and enlisted men, many of whom distinguished themselves during the early fighting in Korea. This work identifies and helps keep the players straight.

063 Summers, Harry G. Jr. Korean War Almanac. New York: Facts on File, 1990.   330 pages, index, illustrations, maps, bibliography.

This brief but informative coverage of major events, and personalities was completed by a well respected historian. The alphabetically listed entries are brief, the information about Inchon is very brief but it is a very useful tool in bringing other works up to date.

064 Thursfield, Henry G. (editor). Brassey's Annual: The Armed Forces Year Book, 1950 - 1954. New York: Macmillan, published annually.

This is a good collection and most helpful because of its listings of both British and Commonwealth units in action during the Korean Conflict. Each annual book offers a new perspective.

065 United States Defense Document Center. Bibliography of Amphibious Operations. Four volumes. Cameron Station, Alexandria, Virginia: Defense Document Center, 1969.

Useful collection of material dealing with various amphibious landings.   Their interpretation of "amphibious" is used in the widest sense, but other than being dated this is a useful source of information.

066   United States Department of the Army. Communist North Korea: A Bibliographic Survey. Washington, DC: Government Printing Office, 1962.
A very selective bibliographical source on the communist government and troops in North Korea. Not only dated but the definition of communism is not clear and listings not well conceived.

ARTICLES

067   Thomas, Robert C.   "The Campaign in Korea" Brassey's Annual: The Armed Forces Yearbook. H. G. Thursfield. (editor). New York: MacMillan, 1953. 222-238.
This annual offering is always a good, brief, source of information on the War. Encyclopedic account of the Korean War; brief, well constructed, concentrated on Inchon.

068   "The War in Korea: Diaries for June 25 - July 30, 1950; August 1 - October 31, 1950" Royal United Service Institution Journal Volume 95 486 - 491, 601 - 611; and volume 96 148 - 155, 298 - 305.
British orientation to the day by day activities of the war, accounting for the first four months. Includes involvement of the British army and navy in the distractions prior to the action at Inchon.

GENERAL HISTORIES OF THE KOREAN WAR

BOOKS

069 Acheson, Dean G. The Korean War. New York: W. W. Norton and Company, 1971. 153 pages, index, illustrations, maps.
This powerful political participant played a central role in the early decision to be involved. He is very critical of the handling of the early phases of the war. He expresses deep concern over MacArthur as both military and diplomatic leader.

070   Alexander, Bevin. Korea: The First War We Lost.
New York: Hippocrene Books, 1986. 558 pages, index,
illustrations, notes, maps.
    Bevin Alexander, Army Combat historian in Korea,
has produced an excellent one volume history. It is one
of the first to make good use of the unpublished
narratives of combat historians, X Corps and Eighth Army
command reports. More than half the work is on the
first year of the war. He attempts to show that the
United States, with the aid of the United Nations,
fought two very different wars. One, with the North
Koreans was won as a result of the Inchon landing, and
second the war with the Chinese, which was lost. He
comes down heavily on the costs of misunderstanding
one's enemies.

071   Appleman, Roy E. The United States Army in the
Korean War: South to the Naktong, North to the Yalu.
Washington, DC: Office of the Chief of Military History,
1961. 813 pages, index, notes, tables, illustrations,
maps.
    The first volume of Appleman's official histories
of the Korean War. These excellent, and very detailed,
accounts provide great background reading. Chapter 25
(488 - 540) deals directly with the Inchon landing and
the re-taking of Seoul. Of particular interest is
Appleman's discussion of the landing controversy.

072   Blair, Clay. The Forgotten War: America in Korea
1950-1953. New York: Times Books, 1987. 1136 pages,
index, maps.
    Blair is a serious historian, and certainly one of
the most prolific, who writes in depth about the Korean
War.   This is an excellent, well researched, and
documented general history. In chapter 10 he deals with
the landing at Inchon, suggesting the victory at Inchon
(267 - 294) was lucky in the face of the odds overcome.

073   Confrontation in Asia: The Korean War. West Point:
Department of History, United States Military Academy,
1981. Index.
    General history text used at the Naval Academy,
excellent map of the Inchon landing.

074 Fehrenbach, T. R. <u>This Kind of War: A Study in
Unpreparedness</u>. New York: Macmillan, 1963. 688 pages,
index, illustrations, maps.
          One of the first general survey histories to
appear. A balanced account of the early war by a man
with some first hand experience. He stresses the fact
of American unpreparedness for limited war and
governmental inability to "get started." A good study,
despite its age, of the tension created by this
political reality. Compiled from post-war interviews.

075 Goulden, Joseph C. <u>Korea: The Untold Story of the
War</u>. New York: McGraw, 1982.   690 pages, index,
illustrations.
          A good standard history in which the author used
the Freedom of Information Act to locate previously
unexplored material.   It is well written and
informative. In discussing the early period of the war,
he sides with, and is strongly supportive of MacArthur
as the Allied commander. The author is one of the few
who deals with "Operation Bluehearts," an early plan to
put the 1st Cavalry Division at Inchon on 22 July, 1950.

076 Halliday, Jon and Bruce Cumings. <u>Korea: The Unknown
War</u>. New York: Pantheon Books, 1988. 224 pages, index,
illustrations, maps.
          One of the better known works, tends to the
dramatic both in word and illustration, but gives one of
the best background looks. The Inchon period is placed
in context but little detailed information provided.

077 Hastings, Max. <u>The Korean War</u>. New York: Simon
and Schuster, 1987.   389 pages, illustrations, maps.
          Hastings, a well respected English military
historian, takes a good look at the Korean War,
recounting the personal experience of the individual
soldiers, as well as the strategies and politics of the
leadership. He covers the period of the Inchon landing
in detail, giving the reader the insights of both a
careful historian, and an observer from the British
point of view. Inchon reflects, he says, the American
"can do" improvisation and risk-taking on a magnificent
scale. 99 - 103.

078 Hoyt, Edwin P. On To the Yalu. New York: Stein and Day, 1984. 297 pages, index, illustrations, notes, maps.

   Good history of the "turn-around" at Inchon and the push north. His treatment of Inchon is one of the few which deals with the KATUSA (Korean Army Troop Augmentation to United States Army) troops who made up a good portion of the 7th Infantry (Army) Division which landed late at Inchon. 17 - 99.

079 Hoyt, Edwin P. Pacific Destiny: The Story of America in the Western Sea from the Early 1800s to the 1980s. New York: W. W. Norton and Company, 1981. 323 pages, index, maps.

   The story of the American presence in the Western sea, this is a long and vastly interesting account. Chapter 30 deals with the Inchon landing and the involvement in the Korean War. Generally such a wide view that it offers little new not well covered elsewhere.

080 Karig, Walter, Malcolm W. Cagle, and Frank A. Manson. Battle Report: The War in Korea. Volume 6. New York: Rinehart and Company, Inc., 1952. 519 pages, index, illustrations, maps, appendix.

   This is an added sixth volume in what was to be a five volume account of World War II by three well qualified historians. The Inchon phase begins with Lt. Clark's mission of reconnaissance and ends with the mop-up of Seoul after the victory there. Appendix contains names of killed and wounded, medals received, and ships of the Inchon landing task force. 176 - 272.

081 Kim, Chum-Kon. The Korean War 1950 - 1953. Seoul, Korea: Kwangmyong Publishing, Ltd. 1973. 604 pages, index, illustrations, maps.

   The author, a Division Commander during the Korean War, provides the Korean point of view, including comment on the "counterattack" (Inchon - 233 - 235). Good source on both North Korean attitudes and actions, but insightful concerning the military utility and movement of the North Korean People's Army. Somewhat dated but useful.

082   Leckie, Robert.   <u>Conflict: The History of the</u>
<u>Korean War, 1950-1953</u>. New York: G. P. Putnam's Sons,
1962. 448 pages, index, illustrations.
     One of the better one volume histories of the War,
out of date by current standards but the basic
information is sound.   Leckie provides good clear
coverage of the Inchon planning, and the "invasion."
125 - 192.

083 Marshall, Samuel L. A. <u>The Military History of the</u>
<u>Korean War</u>. New York: Franklin Watts, Inc. 89 pages,
index, illustrations.
     This is obviously written for young people, but it
is done with Marshall's usual style.   The coverage of
Inchon and the "illusion of victory" is simply and
clearly stated and accompanied by good maps.   This
volume also has some photographs which are not usually
seen.

084   Middleton, Harry J.   <u>The Compact History of the</u>
<u>Korean War</u> New York: Hawthorn Books, Inc. 1965.   255
pages, index, maps.
     One of the better short histories of the Korean
War, with a good chapter on Inchon. Provides insights
on General MacArthur's ability to provide forceful
presentations while avoiding answers to serious
questions.

085 The Ministry of National Defense, The Republic of
Korea. <u>The History of the United Nations Forces in the</u>
<u>Korean War</u>. Five volumes. Seoul, South Korea: Ministry
of National Defense, 1972-1974.   Index, illustrations,
maps.
     Provides the South Korean point of view on the
United Nations forces, and on the military leadership of
the United Nations troops. Is an excellent source of
Korean and United Nations units, action dates,
casualties.   These books are a totally subjective
history of the "three years' fratricidal tragedy"
designed to excuse the excesses of the war.
Acknowledging the contribution of the twenty-one nations
involved in the conflict, it draws attention to the
continuing menace of the communist view.

086 O'Ballance, Edgar. <u>Korea 1950-53</u>. London: Faber,
1969. 171 pages, map, bibliography.
    This brief history contains a chapter on Inchon in
which the author concentrates on the "hair raising"
gamble. Every logical consideration, as well as most
military leaders, were against the attempt. But, after
all is said and done, it worked. 30 - 56.

087 Rees, David. <u>Korea: The Limited War</u>. New York:
St. Martin's Press, 1964.   511   pages,   index,
illustrations, appendix, bibliography.
    Still one of the best histories of the Korean War,
the author combines political and military history in a
unique manner. His discussion of Inchon (The Impossible
Victory) is excellent, and his emphasis on the second
phase, the Seoul campaign, is one of the best overviews
available. Inchon, he concluded, was a plan which could
only be carried out by MacArthur. 77 - 99.

088 Rees, David. (editor). <u>The Korean War: History and
Tactics</u>. New York: Crescent, 1984. 128 pages, index,
illustrations.
    Good volume of the war's military aspects. Best
treatment of policy in relation to military operations.
Supportive and considers "American involvement in Korea,
the greatest act in recent American history."

089 Ridgway, Matthew B. <u>The Korean War</u>. Garden City,
New York: Doubleday, 1967. 192 pages, index, maps.
    While Ridgway arrived late to Korea, his
participation in the decision to land at Inchon was an
important one. His comments on the decision, and on the
landing, are significant.

090 Sandusky, Michael. <u>America's Parallel</u>. Alexandria,
Virginia: Old Dominion Press, 1983. 420 pages, index,
illustrations, maps, bibliography.
    A carefully constructed history of the conflict
(rather than the war) in Korea as seen in its largest
context. The author tells us more than most want to
know about "crisp salutes" and who borrowed whose
clothing, but there is a good discussion of Inchon in
"its larger context." 264 - 282.

091 Schnabel, James F. <u>The United States Army in the Korean War, Policy and Direction: The First Year</u>. Washington, DC: Office of the Chief of Military History, 1968, 1972. Index, illustrations, maps.

This essential work, the second volume of the five projected volumes of the United States Army and the Korean War Series. Chapters 8 and 9 (138 - 172) provide a detailed account of the planning and execution of Operation Chromite. This is an excellent resource. Very detailed, significantly footnoted, with valuable analysis.

092 Stokesbury, James L. <u>A Short History of the Korean War</u>. New York: Quill, William Morrow, 1988. 276 pages, index, maps.

This volume, one in a series of "Short Histories," is well done, but has all the problems of a brief history. The tone of this work is the inevitability of the United States involvement in Korea once military action began. He does a good job of putting Inchon into context.   "Not perhaps one of history's decisive battles...but a classic military operation." (15) Contains an excellent analysis of the military commanders involved.

093 Stone, Isidor F. <u>The Hidden History of the Korean War</u>. New York: Monthly Review Press, 1952. 364 pages, index, references.

This is still one of the more controversial works on the war, even though published before the war was over. Stone, a well known liberal journalist introduces the United States--Republic of Korea conspiracy, placing much of the blame for the war on the United States. He saw military courage at Inchon but not political responsibility.

094 Taylor, Maxwell D. <u>The Uncertain Trumpet</u>. New York: Harper, 1959. 203 pages.

General Maxwell Taylor, who was the United States Army Chief of Staff and Commander of the Eighth Army during the final period, is critical of the United States running of the Korean War, and of the early phase.

095   Thomas, Robert C. <u>The War in Korea</u>.   Aldershot, England: Gale, 1954.
     While this book was written very early and without benefit of the numerous recent studies and analysis, this British officer/historian provides a good general survey and strong support for both the United Nations involvement, and for General MacArthur's handling of the war.

096 Thompson, Reginald. <u>Cry Korea</u>.   London: Macdonald and Company (Publishers) Ltd., 1951.   301 pages, index, illustrations.
     British correspondent who went along on the Inchon landing, considered the whole effort to be over-kill, too much force for too little target.   Thompson found the marines to be less humane than he expected.   An interesting affirmation of the British view that they were fighting in Korea, but not for Korea.   Inchon landing covered 19 - 96.

097 Toland, John. <u>In Mortal Combat: 1950 - 1953</u>. New York: William Morrow and Company, 1991.   624 pages, index, illustrations, maps.
     This popular historian has produced a sound history of the Korean War.   It is weakened by his recreation of situations and dialogue where there is little historical support for his renderings.   Short anecdotes appear for little reason other than to liven up the story.   But he has been one of the few writers to locate and use detailed North Korean and Chinese sources and that gives it a view generally unexpected.   His analysis appears overly harsh on the United States and there appears to be some key omissions.   Inchon, he entitles, "It's a piece of cake!"

098 Whelan, Richard. <u>Drawing the Line: The Korean War, 1950 - 1953</u>. Boston: Little, Brown, and Company, 1990. 428 pages, index, illustrations, maps.
     Fairly good general history with a chapter dealing with the problems, and victories, at Inchon.   Includes a discussion of MacArthur's charismatic, rather than military, leadership; and his dependence on Wolfe's tactics for the Inchon concept.

ARTICLE

099 Farrar, Peter N. "A Pause for Peace Negotiations:
The British Buffer Zone Plan of November 1950" in James
Cotton and Ian Neary. The Korean War in History.
[Studies on East Asia]. Atlantic Highlands, New Jersey:
Humanities Press International, Inc., 1989. 66 - 79.
     One   of   a   collection   of   revisionist's
interpretations which sees the War in terms of domestic
actions, and which saw the Inchon landing and drive
toward China as the essential end of the War. Failure
to consider the British plan seriously led to a whole
new war.

HISTORIOGRAPHIC

BOOK

100 Cotton, James and Ian Neary. The Korean War in
History. Atlantic Highland, New Jersey: Humanities
Press International, Inc., 1989. 187 pages, index.
     A look at the way history as a discipline has
recorded the Korean War, Inchon being an example of the
selected coverage.

ARTICLES

101 Foot, Rosemary. "Historiography: Making Known the
Unknown War: Policy Analysis of the Korean Conflict in
the Last Decade" Diplomatic History 15:3 (Summer
1991) 411 - 431.
     An excellent account of the ex post facto histories
of the Korean War (including Inchon) but particularly
interesting in terms of the "meaning" of the first phase
of the war. This fine historian has provided a good
1990s look at the Korean War and the bibliographic
interpretations of it. While not specifically on the
Inchon landing, any attempt to understand, or produce
current interpretation requires the reading of this
essay.

102   Swartout, R. Jr.   "American Historians and the Outbreak of the Korean War: An Historiographical Essay" Asia Quarterly [Belgium]   (1979)   65 - 77.
    Swartout provides several schools of thought on who started, and was responsible, for the war. Leading contenders: MacArthur, Syngman Rhee, USSR, and Kim Il Sung.

THE INCHON DEBATE

BOOKS

103   Barham, Pat and Frank Cunningham.   Operation Nightmare: The Story of America's Betrayal in Korea and the United Nations.   Los Angeles: Sequoia University Press, 1953.   350 pages, index, illustrations.
    Generally an expose of the United Nations failures and a strong support of General Douglas MacArthur "our great   living   general   and   American,   a   victim   of governmental blundering and treason. . . " Barham, a war correspondent who was a participant, discusses Inchon only as a part of the greater failure. 13 - 23, 185, 214, 308, 340.

104   Heinl, Robert D. Jr.   Victory at High Tide: The Inchon-Seoul Campaign.   New York: J. B. Lippincott, 1968.   315 pages, index, illustrations, maps.
    The best work on the Inchon period, Heinl (a Marine Corps officer) is a little prejudice toward the Corp, but has produced an excellent work. If only one volume was available on Inchon, this is it. MacArthur was not convinced that the landing at Inchon would be sufficient for the Eighth Army to break out of Pusan and move north. He felt that General Walker and the defenders of Pusan had been retreating so long they might be unable to take the offensive even if the Inchon attack was successful.   Therefore, MacArthur suggested other possible landings (147 - 148) to break the hold, the replacement of Walker as Army Commander (246 - 248), as well as lack of confidence in Eighth Army in general (246 - 256).   Events were to prove MacArthur wrong.

105   Hopkins, William B.   One Bugle No Drums: The Marines at Chosin Reservoir. Chapel Hill: Algonquin Books, 1986. 274 pages, maps, index, bibliography, appendix.

Hopkins provides essentially a book about the fight at Chosin, which goes well beyond this inquiry, but chapter 3 contains a very good account of the formation of the marine units which landed at Wolmi-do and then Inchon. Marines were arriving at Inchon from all over, down to the last minute. The 7th Regiment was put together from marines serving on ships of the 6th Fleet in the Mediterranean, and did not arrive in time for the first wave of those landing at Inchon. When they did arrive, they served admirably at Inchon and continued on to Seoul and finally Chosin.

106   James, D. Clayton and Anne S. Wells. Refighting the Last War: Command and Crisis in Korea, 1950-1953. New York: Free Press, 1993.   282 pages, index, illustrations.

The authors claim that the Korean War was not only fought with equipment and materials left over from World War II, but that the strategic and tactical doctrines used were also left over from the previous war. They find no better example of this than the Inchon landing. The decision for and execution of the amphibious operation was described as MacArthur's supreme act of refighting the last war. Chapter 7 "MacArthur's Grand Obsession: Inchon" investigates this thesis in considerable detail.

107   Kaufman, Burton I.   The Korean War: Challenges in Crisis, Credibility, and Command. Philadelphia: Temple University Press, 1986.   381 pages, index, map.

Primarily a book about the politics of international conflict. However, chapter 3 discusses the period of the United Nations offensive, and looks at the Inchon landing from its political implication. One interesting comment suggests that the successful landing played a role in the political agenda and, as it turned out, provided the background for the replacement of Louis Johnson, the conservative's favorite defense secretary.

108   MacDonald, Callum A.   Korea: The War Before
Vietnam. New York: The Free Press (Macmillan, Inc.),
1986. 330 pages, index.
    Obviously an attempt to relate the two Asian wars.
Whether successful in this effort, it is a useful source
because of the discussion (chapter 4) of what Dean
Acheson identified as MacArthur's "mirage of total
victory." While MacArthur turned the victory at Inchon
into an excuse for overriding the limitations of his
military directive from the United Nations, he did so
either with Washington's backing, or in their ignorance.

109 Mortensen, Roger. Inchon and the Strategy of the
Indirect Approach.   Air Command and Staff College,
Research Report, Maxwell Air Force Base, Alabama, 1977.
42 pages.
    A student special project report from the command
classes at the Air Command and Staff College, responding
to the question of interdiction. A copy is available at
the Air University Library, but only to qualified
scholars and with special permission from the staff.

110   Quigley, John.   The Ruses for War: American
Interventionism Since World War II. Buffalo, New York:
Prometheus Books, 1992. 310 pages, index, bibliography.
    Chapters 2, 3, and 4 deal with the pressures on
America for entry into the Korean War. Quigley's thesis
is that fear of Russian intervention served both to lead
us into war, and limit us once we were in it. Discussion
of the "internationalization" of the Inchon landing.

111 Ridgway, Matthew B. The Korean War: History and
Tactics. Garden City, New York: Doubleday and Company,
1967. 268 pages, index, illustrations, maps, appendix.
    While General Matthew B. Ridgway came late to Korea
he had a greater understanding of it than many military
leaders.   In this work he covers the war from the
beginning. During this early phase Ridgway was doing
planning and was, in a real sense, Chief of Staff for
Korea. He visited MacArthur to try and stop the Inchon
landing, but was won over. His assessment of the Inchon
argument and conditions at Inchon are very significant.
30 - 42.

112   Schnabel, James F. and Robert G. Watson.   History
of the Joint Chiefs of Staff: The Joint Chiefs of Staff
and National Policy.   Volume 3. Washington, DC: History
Division, part 1 - 1978, part 2 - 1979.
      Contains   a   significant   amount   of   information
dealing with the planning, and execution of war policy
during the Korean War.   Produced in soft cover and
duplicated   by   the   Historical   Division,   Joint
Secretariat, Joint Chiefs of Staff, it is available
through Modern Military History Headquarters, National
Archives.

113 Traverso, Edmond. (compiler).   Korea and the Limits
of Limited War.   Menlo Park, California: Addison-Wesley
Publisher, 1970.   81 pages, maps.
      This collection of documents on the Korean War
contains General MacArthur's statement, concerning the
landing at, and following the action, of Inchon.   One of
the primary concerns, other than the success of the
landing, was what to do if it worked and the North
Korean Army folded as anticipated.   This statement was
made the day before the landing but for some reason was
not released until 5 May 1951.   Also contains the Joint
Chiefs of Staff directive to MacArthur on the day of the
landing.

ARTICLES

114 Bhagat, B. S.   "Military Lessons of the Korean War"
The Journal of the United Service Institution of India
(January - April, 1952)   5 - 21.   [Reprinted in
Military   Review,   Command   and   Staff   College,
Leavenworth, Kansas 32:9 (December 1952).
      This article discusses military lessons learned
during each phase of the war.   Inchon, considered as
phase two, taught the value of a unified supreme
command; acknowledged the fact intelligence was very
poor;   and   stressed   the   value   of   inter-service
cooperation at Inchon where the United Nations Army,
Navy, Marines and the Air Wings all worked together for
a victory.

115 Carpenter, Ronald H. "General Douglas MacArthur's Oratory on Behalf of Inchon" Southern Communication Journal 58:1 (Fall 1992) 1 - 12.

This collection is obviously more concerned with the oratory than the contents but it provides a good source of General MacArthur's obvious ability to use words to achieve his purposes. The author writes in detail about the assumptions on which Inchon was selected.

116 Halloran, B. F. "Inchon Landing" Marine Corps Gazette 56:9 (September 1972) 25 - 32.

A very supportive statement concerning the planning and execution of the Inchon landing which the author felt was not only "masterful," but was accomplished in record time. The author's excellent account states that the landing was the most "dramatic transition from defense to attack in the annals of war." A practical response to the comment "amphibious operations are a thing of the past."

117 Heinl, Robert D. "The Inchon Landing: A Case Study in Amphibious Planning" Naval War College Review 39:9 (Summer 1967) 51 - 72.

Heinl includes some materials which would later be published in his very fine book-length study. A good account by this top historian on the full range of planning and execution of Operation Chromite. He supports Admiral W. F. Halsey's statement "the Inchon landing is the most masterly and audacious strategic stroke in all history."

118 "The Korean War" Newsweek 36:13 (September 25, 1950) 21 - 30.

This article contains an outline and analysis of the Inchon landing. It was "the most telegraphed Sunday punch in military history" (21) but was still successful. Several other landing sites were suggested and discussed. This article is an excellent source on diversion efforts at the areas of Kunsan, Mokpo, Samchok, Yongdok and Pohang. Contains some very fine detailed maps for the landing, including the various beaches.

119   Larew, Karl G. "Inchon Invasion Not a Stroke of Genius or Even Necessary" Army 38 (December 1988) 15 - 20.

Larew contends that the strike at Inchon did not save the Eighth Army, for it was not in danger. It would have been better to use the 1st Marine Division to support the Eighth. The decision at Inchon put Pusan in danger as they pulled troops out. The victory at Inchon led to the invasion of the North because it made Truman and MacArthur think they could not be beaten. Larew contends that the President should have stopped MacArthur's plan.

120   Lavine, Harold.   "Inchon: 'A HelluvaGamble' that Paid Off" Newsweek 36:13 (September 25, 1950) 25.

Lavine, one of the first newsman to land with the Marines describes the high risks involved in making the landing at all and expresses amazement at the early success.

121   "The MacArthur Story" U. S. News and World Report 30 (May 11, 1951) 52 - 64; 30 (May 18, 1951) 52 - 66+.

Report of hearings conducted before the Senate Armed Services Committee, concerning MacArthur's actions, and the decision to release him. Contains some materials on the Inchon decision.

122   Pirnie, Bruce R.   "The Inchon Landing: How Great Was the Risk?" Joint Perspectives 3:1 (Summer 1982) 86 - 97.

The author gives an excellent review of the landing at Inchon, then concludes that it was not really much of a gamble. The situation was such that "periculum in mora" (danger in delay).

123   Schnabel, James F. "The Inchon Landing: Perilous Gamble or Exemplary Boldness?" Army 9 (May 1959) 50.

An excellent account of the planning, risks, evaluation of the Inchon landing, which is generally supportive of General MacArthur, his planning staff, and the decisiveness of the battle which led to eventual victory.

124   Smith, Lynn D. "A Nickel After a Dollar: MacArthur's Daring Plan for the Invasion of Inchon" Army 20 (September 1970) 24.
General Lynn Smith was the officer who MacArthur trusted to brief the Joint Chiefs of Staff on the details of the Inchon landing plan. The analogy, supposedly MacArthur's, was that the landing at Inchon was but a nickel (thrown in the pot of the Korean War) while the dollar was the decision to involve American troops in the war.

125   Spaatz, Carl.   "General MacArthur Read General Wolfe" Newsweek 36:15 (October 9, 1950) 26 - 27.
Spaatz relates that General MacArthur had drawn deeply in his historical background and knowledge, and that MacArthur had conceived his idea about Inchon, following "in the footsteps as Wolfe at Quebec . . . It was the answer to the problem." This is a seeming illusion which some have attributed to MacArthur himself.

126   "Tokyo-Washington Messages Behind Dismissal of MacArthur" U. S. News and World Report 30 (April 20, 1951) 46 - 49.
A brief account of, and excerpts from, messages passing back and forth between Washington and Tokyo concerning the administration's policy. The messages quickly show that MacArthur had indeed violated the assumed policy. There are some interesting Inchon comments, concerning the landing.

127   Tomlinson, H. Pat.   "Inchon: The General's Decision" Military Review 47 (April 1967) 28 - 35.
This article centers on the Joint Chiefs of Staff debate over approval of the landing, the alternative landings suggested (one site suggested was Kunsan), and relates the landing to Wolfe at Quebec. A concept which appears with great regularity in accounts of the Inchon landing. The Joint Chiefs of Staff were overwhelmed by MacArthur who outranked and out demanded them all. A detailed account of the plans for the amphibious invasion of Inchon and the recapture of Seoul as it was envisioned by MacArthur.

128   Totten, James P. "Operation Chromite: A Study in Generalship" <u>Armor</u> 85 (November-December, 1976) 33 - 38.

The entire operation at the Inchon landing was conceived, staffed, and executed within 90 days.   In order to put the plan into operation, foreign nationals serving in the United States 7th Infantry Division, untrained ship captains and inexperienced crews, Japanese nationals and their landing craft were involved in pulling it off. The author argues that the operation was unjustified on every grounds but imagination. But, once it was decided, an amazing job was performed.

129   "Turning of the Tide in Korea and the Meeting of 'a New Foe'"   <u>United Nations Bulletin</u> 9:10 (November 15, 1950) 528 - 530.

This contains excerpts from MacArthur's report to the United Nations on the landing at Inchon, and the associated successful campaign against Seoul. Somewhere between the tide tables and his own "sense" of timing it was generally accepted that..."had the landing been delayed so much as a month, it would have been too late."   Or, it might even well be argued, totally unnecessary.

130   "War in Asia" <u>Time</u> 56:13 (September 25, 1950) 25 - 32.

In reporting, the landing at Inchon was described as being in the "American tradition."   Maps and descriptions are very good, particularly of Wolmi-do island and a good account of three leaders; General Almond, Admiral Struble, and Admiral Doyle: the X Corps and 7th Task Force commanders.

131   "We Weren't Permitted to Win in Korea" <u>U. S. News and World Report</u> 37 (September 3, 1954) 81 - 84.

General Stratmeyer testifies before the Senate Armed Services Committee telling them that General "MacArthur's hands were tied" when it came to his dealings both political and military. Nothing new as far as information, but carefully arranged to show support for General MacArthur.

132 Wilz, John E.   "The MacArthur Inquiry, 1951." in Arthur Schlesinger and Roger Burns (editors). Congress Investigates: A Documental History 1792-1974. Volume 5. New York: Chelsea House, 1975.   3592 - 3727.
An account of the politics behind MacArthur's dismissal, the reasons behind it, all very well supported by a collection of pertinent documents and a bibliographic essay.

THE LANDING

Ground

BOOKS

133 Aguirre, Emilio. We'll Be Home For Christmas: A True Story of the United States Marine Corps in the Korean War. New York: Greenwich, 1959.
The exploits of a marine from Company G, 3rd Battalion, 7th Marines who took part in the Inchon landing and went on to take part in the Chosin Reservoir retreat.

134 Anderson, Kenneth. U. S. Military Operations: 1945-1983. New York: The Military Press, 1984.   192 pages, index, illustrations.
General illustrated history but has a good section on Inchon including a well defined map of the Inchon-Seoul campaign. 41 - 44.

135 Bartlett, Norman. With the Australians in Korea. Canberra, Australia: Australia War Memorial, 1954. Index.
The Australians sent an air force contingency in July of 1950, and eventually had forces on the ground (with the Commonwealth Brigade), in the air (77th Squadron), and at sea (destroyer Bataan, frigate Shoalhaven, and HMAS Warramunga, a destroyer, HMAS Sydney, HMAS Condamine, and Murchison. The new Zealand ship Pukaki was at Inchon.

136   Brainard, Morgan.   <u>Then They Called For The Marines: A Marine Rifle Company in Korea, 1950-1951</u>. Rutland, Vermont: Academy Books, 1989. 2nd edition. Formerly published as <u>Men in Low Cut Shoes</u>.

A rather standard account of the men in a rifle company, from the marine landing past the Seoul campaign.

137   Carew, Tim.   <u>Korea: The Commonwealth at War</u>. London: Cassell, 1967.   307 pages, index, illustrations.

British forces were in the Korean War from the beginning, but ground forces came in late August.   At Inchon the Woolworth Brigade was in the follow-up landings and moved with United Nations forces toward Seoul and beyond.   The British involvement was small, but their record in action was significant.

138   David, Alan A. (editor).   Seventh Infantry Division, Public Information Office. <u>Bayonet: A History of the 7th Infantry Division in Korea</u>. Tokyo: Dai Nippon, 1953.

A somewhat exaggerated administrative history of the 7th (Hourglass) Infantry Division from its involvement in the summer of 1950 to the end of 1952. The 7th landed on the second day at Inchon, and moved against Seoul.

139   Farrar-Hockley, Anthony.   <u>The British Part in the Korean War: A Distant Obligation</u>.   Volume 1.   London: His Majesty's Stationary Office, 1990.   512 pages, index, illustrations, maps, appendix.

An excellent work by this British participant-historian.   Deals with the British involvement in the Inchon landing, most of which was naval and all related to diversionary tactics.   Appendix L is the best listing to locate specific commanders, ships, and duties. British forces were involved in several deception attempts during the Inchon landing, and naval forces provided deception duties near Kunsan.   Inchon is discussed under the heading (chapter 7) "A Stroke of Genius" which seems to give the author's opinion of the operation.   The maps are well drawn and printed and give a careful picture of the forces involved.   143 - 158.

140   Geer, Andrew.   The New Breed, The Story of the U. S. Marines in Korea.   New York: Harper and Brothers, 1952.   395 pages, index, maps.
This is the story of the United States Marines in Korea.   While the Marines came late to the campaign in Korea, early August 1950, their presence made a considerable difference both in terms of morale and number of fighting men.   Once in Korea, and holding their sector of the Pusan Perimeter, the Marines were pulled out of the Pusan area, regrouped, and shipped to Inchon.   They were the major fighting force at Inchon landing, and a major factor in the success of the Seoul campaign.   Chapters 8, 9, and 10 deal with the landing at Inchon.

141   Grey, Jeffrey.   The Commonwealth Armies and the Korean War: An Alliance Study.   New York: Manchester University   Press,   1988.   244   pages,   index, illustrations, maps.
Grey, a well respected British historian, deals throughout with individual commonwealth nations, and commonwealth units, including in, around, and following the Inchon landing.   The most impressive aspects of this work, however, lie in the appendix, a careful listing of units involved, and in the wide bibliographical and archival sources listed for both Commonwealth and American materials.

142   Heinl, Robert D.   Soldiers of the Sea: The United States Marine Corps, 1775-1962.   Annapolis, Maryland: United States Naval Institute, 1962.   692 pages, index, illustrations, appendix with corps strengths.
An excellent one volume history of the United States Marine Corps.   Obviously written in support of the Marine corps -- and in support of their continued existence in the face of opposition -- but nevertheless an informative account of the Marines many actions successfully carried out, including the landing at Inchon.   The author uses this work to accuse a wide variety of persons with trying to get rid of the marines, for a variety of political, as well as military reasons, but does provide a good general history including Inchon.   547 - 562.

143   Historical Division, 7th Infantry. <u>Bayonet: A History of the 7th Infantry Division</u>. Tokyo: Toppan Printing Company, Ltd., 1952. 75 pages, illustration, maps.
     An early publication designed for the new troops assigned to the division. Has a history of each organizational unit, including those who landed at Inchon. Contains a TO&E for the division at the time it landed.

144   Langley, Michael. <u>Inchon Landing: MacArthur's Last Triumph</u>. New York: Times Books, 1979. 182 pages, index, illustrations, bibliography, maps.
     A British account of the preparations for, and execution of, the Inchon landing. Brief and overly simple at times, it nevertheless is strongly supportive of MacArthur and the landing that was "an amazing example of planning, luck, courage, and leadership."

145   Montross, Lynn and Nicholas A. Canzona. <u>U. S. Marine Operations in Korea, 1950 - 1953</u>. Volume 2. <u>Inchon-Seoul Operation</u>. Washington, DC: Government Printing Office, 1955. 361 pages, index, illustrations, maps, appendix.
     A moment by moment narrative of the Marine landings at Inchon. An excellent account by two distinguished military historians. Appendix includes lists of units involved, officers, ships, etc.

146   Murphy, Jack. <u>History of the US Marines</u>. New York: Exter   Books,   1984.   224   pages,   index, illustrations.
     A general illustrated history which deals with the Korean experience (chapter 5) and provides a very good description of the marine aspects of the Inchon landing, all supported with illustrations.

147   O'Neill, Robert. <u>Australia in the Korean War</u>. Volume 1. Canberra, Australia: The Australian War Memorial and Australian Government Publishing Service, 1981.
     Deals with the commitment of Australian naval, air, and ground troops, June 1950 - July 1953. 1 - 77.

148 Reserve Officers of Public Affairs Unit 4-1. The Marine Corps Reserve: A History. Washington, DC: Division of Reserve, Headquarters, US Marine Corps, 1966. 311 pages, index, illustrations.
    Chapter 8, "Korea" (164 - 180) deals with the efforts to rebuild the Marine Corps in time to respond to General MacArthur's call for a Marine division. It was necessary to dig deeply into the reserve system to meet the demand for troops. This work is a general history of the reserves but its chapter on the recall for the Korean War, and the immediate involvement of reserves in combat, is a strong argument in favor of a ready reserve.

149 Stanton, Shelby L. America's Tenth Legion: X Corps in Korea, 1950. Novato, California: Presidio Press, 1989. 342 pages, index, illustrations, maps.
    A better than average look at X Corps, its commander, its assignments, and the difficulties raised by the complicated command and unusual assignments. Does a nice job looking at the creation of X corps, its planning and execution of the Inchon landing, and follow through. The creation of the independent body, and its separate existence on the drive north, was one of the more controversial issues of MacArthur's command.

150 Thorgrimsson, Thor and E. C. Russell. Canadian Naval Operations in Korean Waters, 1950-1955. Ottawa: Department of National Defense, Canadian Forces, HQ Naval Historical Section, 1965.
    Canada made a good initial response to the Korean War. This is an accounting of Canadian forces which fought with the United Nations during the war, including the presence of destroyers at Inchon.

151 United States Military Academy, Department of Military Art and Engineering. Operations in Korea. West Point, New York: United States Military Academy, 1956.
    A brief, but fairly inclusive, account of American military units in Korea. The work includes those units which were operational during, and their movements at the Inchon landing.

152   United   States   Operations   Research   Office.
<u>Integration of ROK Soldiers into U. S. Army Units</u>
<u>(KATUSA)</u>. Washington, DC: Government Printing Office,
1990. 125 pages.
      The KATUSA project brought on many critics, but it
made possible the 7th Division (Army) landing at Inchon
and then contributed to the battle of Seoul.

153   Wilson, Jim.   <u>Retreat, Hell! We're Just Attacking</u>
<u>in Another Direction</u>.   New York: William Morrow and
Company, Inc, 1988. 349 pages, illustrations.
      A classic account of the Marine retreat from
Chosin, but he does begin with a highly informative
account of the landing of Marines at Inchon.   Worth
reading chapter 1.

ARTICLES

154   Balmforth, Ed. E.   "Getting Our ROKS Off" <u>Combat</u>
<u>Forces Journal</u> 1:7 (1951) 22 - 25.
      Discusses the decision to add more than a thousand
Republic of Korea soldiers into the 17th Infantry
Regiment of the 7th Division (Army) prior to the 7th
administrative landing at Inchon.   While the division
was under-strength and needed help this article is
critical of the manner in which it was done.

155   Blumenson, Martin.   "MacArthur's Divided Command"
<u>Army</u>   7   (November 1956)   38 - 44, 65.
      Considers the reasons for, and the reasons against,
the creation of a divided command in Korea.   The
creation of X Corps for the Inchon landing may have been
brilliant, according to some, though it created some
serious logistic problems as well as command confusion.
But the failure to unite commands after the fall of
Seoul was not wise.

156   Braitsch, Fred, Jr.   "The Korean Marine Corps"
<u>Leatherneck</u> 36:1 (1953) 30 - 33.
      The Republic of Korea Marines were participants in
the Inchon landing, and are discussed briefly in this
account, acting both as diversionary forces and in the
attack on Kimpo.

157   Chung, Ul Mun. "Letter From Almond" <u>Leatherneck</u>
36:4 (1953) 34 - 35.
    A Korean interpreter comments on his early months
with the 7th Marines who arrived in time for the Inchon
to Seoul phase.

158   Coggins, Thomas M.   "Replacements Are Coming"
<u>Marine Corps Gazette</u> 37:6 (1953) 50 - 54.
    When the Korean War broke out the marines were in
what amounted to a layoff. The sudden call for the 1st
Marine Division reserve, the recall to Camp Pendleton,
California, turned it into a beehive of replacement and
training.

159   Conner, John.   "The New Breed" <u>Collier's</u>   126
(1950) 71 - 72.
    Accounts for the 1st Marine Brigade during the
first two months of the Korean War, including time along
the defensive lines of the Pusan Perimeter, and the
pull-out for the Inchon landing.

160   Dill, James.   "Winter of the Yalu" <u>American
Heritage</u> 34 (1982) 33 - 48.
    A member of the Army 7th Division he accounts the
landing at Inchon in September, then to the Yalu and
back. One of the few commentaries on the 7th Division
at Inchon.

161   Edwards, Spencer P. Jr. "KATUSA--An Experiment in
Korea" <u>United States Naval Institute Proceedings</u> 84:1
(January 1958) 31 - 37.
    A pretty good look at the KATUSA effort and the
role of the 7th Infantry Division which served as
trainer and host division. The KATUSA did better than
expected, but were not without difficulty as a military
unit. More than 7000 were attached to the 7th prior to
the Inchon landing.

162   Eldredge, Jim.   "End of the Beginning" <u>Soldiers</u>
40 (September 1985) 6 - 8.
    Very little new or unusual. A general account of
the landing which claims that it was the turning point
of the war. "The gamble paid off -- in aces."

163 Heinl, Robert D. "Inchon" Marine Corps Gazette
51 (September 1967) 20 - 28, and (October 1967) 45 -
50.
A two-part in-depth account of the planning, Marine
preparation and shipments as well as the landing.
Center to this study is the author's wonder at
MacArthur's division of the landing to a morning attack
on Wolmi-do and an afternoon attack on Inchon. Must be
considered a masterpiece of planning. An analysis of
the materials which he would later publish in
considerably more detail in book form.

164 "Inchon: The Beachhead for Professionals" Marine
Corps Gazette 69 (September 1985) 3 - 6.
MacArthur knew the Marines and what they could do,
so he called for the 1st Division to land at Inchon.
The whole thing was beautifully planned, supported and
executed. The reason it looked so simple, according to
General O. P. Smith was "that professionals did it."

165 Jeung, U. H. "ROK Marines: Battle Hardened Heroes"
Korean Survey 6:8 (1957) 6.
The ROK Marine Corp was activated in 1949 and,
after initial training, were active in the Inchon
invasion, and the attack on Seoul. Though small they
played an important role in the landing.

166 Jones, James C. "Recall"   Leatherneck   34:11
(1951) 14 - 21.
When the call went out for the 1st Marine Division,
the best hope lay in the qualified reserves who could
be, and were, recalled for immediate active duty.

167 Mainard, Allen G. "Sea Wall" in Karl Schuon
(editor). The Leatherneck: An Informal History of the
U. S. Marines. New York: Franklin Watts, Inc., 1993.
231 - 235.
An excellent (and personal) account of the marines
hitting the sixteen foot harbor sea wall which protected
Inchon and which had to be scaled by the landing troops.
It marked a historic moment for the Marines. Original
article located in Mainard, Allen G. "Sea Wall"
Leatherneck 40:9 (1957) 42 - 45.

168   "Marine Muscle Heads into War: 1st Division Men Sail for Korea" <u>Life</u> 29 (July 24, 1950) 28 - 29.
     Really a cover story of the first marines - the Provisional Brigade - as they head out. The Division came later.

169   Montross, Lynn. "Fleet Marine Force Korea, I" <u>United States Naval Institute Proceedings</u> 79:8 (August 1953) 829-841.
     First part of a two part account of the marines in Korea. This first section contains a detailed account of the preparations for, and the execution of, the landing at Inchon and the Kimpo/Seoul campaign. Second part in 79:9 (September 1953) 995, continues to Hungnam.

170 Montross, Lynn. "The Inchon Landing: Victory Over Time and Tide" <u>Marine Corps Gazette</u> 35:7 (July 1951) 26 - 35.
     This is a very significant article. It deals with the reversal in Marine Corps history, when MacArthur requests a Marine division. This necessitated the call up of troops, organization for reservists, transportation of whole units to Japan and Korea, the planning and supply of a division, the landing at Inchon, and the assault on Seoul.

171 Parry, Francis F. "Marine Artillery in Korea: Part I, Ready or Not" <u>Marine Corps Gazette</u> 71:6 (June 1987) 47 - 52.
     Brief memoirs of a man who was a battalion commander of a marine artillery outfit. Researchers often forget that the marines provided much of their own artillery support.

172 Skaggs, David C. "The KATUSA Experiment: The Integration of Korean Nationals into the U. S. Army, 1950-1965" <u>Military Affairs</u> 38:2 (April 1974) 53 - 58.
     The author considered the experiment a disaster and, as a military effort, a failure. The only thing it accomplished for the 7th Infantry Division was to fill up its ranks, but even that did not prove to be combat effective.

173   Smith Oliver P.   "Inchon Landing" <u>Marine Corps</u>
<u>Gazette</u> 44 (September 1960) 40 - 41.
     Written by the commanding general of the 1st Marine
Division, and this is his only comment on the war. He
indicated amazement at the ability of the navy and
marines to land a combat ready division on the beaches
in such a short time with so little difficulty.
Provides details of 1st Marine Division Operation order
(02-50) the Inchon Landing Operational Plan. For a
landing which they were unable to rehearse it went very
well, ending up only slightly behind schedule.

174   Stickney, William W.   "The Marine Reserves in
Action" <u>Military Affairs</u> 17:1 (Spring 1953) 16 - 22.
     The Marine Corps had been allowed to be divided a
great deal so, when MacArthur called for the 1st Marine
Division it was necessary to quickly rebuild the Corps.
This is the story of that mobilization (including the
recall) of marine reserves during the early stages of
the Korean War. Nearly 50 per cent of all officers and
men recalled and mobilized were essentially combat
ready, and 2881 were immediately assigned to the 1st
Marine Division.

175   Tallent, Robert W.   "Pusan -- A Stop Enroute"
<u>Leatherneck</u> 33 (1950) 14 - 17.
     Traces the pull-out of the 1st Provisional Marines
who in the midst of a desperate fight to save Pusan,
but, on MacArthur's orders, were pulled out in the
middle of the fight to prepare for the Inchon landing.
At a time when the success of the defense was in serious
question, and against Walker's requests, MacArthur
pulled the marines out, regrouped, and went on to the
invasion.

176   Tapplet, R. D. and R. E. Whipple. "Darkhorse Sets
the Pace" <u>Marine Corps Gazette</u> 37:6:7 (June-July 1950)
14 - 23, 44 - 50. Maps, views.
     The United States 1st Marine Division carried the
landing at Inchon. The spearheaded group was the Third
Battalion, Fifth Marines Regiment. This is an account
of the combat activities of the Third Battalion at the
Inchon landing.

Air

BOOKS

177 Brown, David. The Seafire: The Spitfire that Went
to Sea. Annapolis, Maryland: Naval Institute Press,
1989. 208 pages, index, illustrations, bibliography.
     Covers in part three, the British role in
deception, bombardment and spotting during the Inchon
campaign when this ocean going spitfire saw considerable
action.

178 Cooling, Benjamin F.   Case Studies in the
Development of Close Air Support.   Washington, DC:
Office of United States Air Force History, 1990.   606
pages, index, illustrations.
     Discusses the development and execution of close
air-ground support missions which include some insights
into the problems of unified or identified command, and
inter-service problems. 367 - 382

179 Doll, Thomas E. USN/USMC Over Korea. Carrollton,
Texas: Squadron/Signal Publications, 1988.   64 pages,
illustrations, maps.
     Essentially a picture book of planes involved in
the United States Navy and Marine Corps flyers in Korea,
but includes a good detailed account of sorties over
Inchon. 9 - 24.

180 Futrell, Robert F. The United States Air Force in
Korea, 1950-1953. New York: Duell, Sloan and Pearce,
1961. Revised edition, 1983.   774 pages, index,
illustrations, maps, notes.
     Considers the air war in Korea as an example of
what not to do next time.   Futrell, of the Air
University, deals with the transition between more
conventional warfare and jets.   A good and factual
history of the recreation of the Far East Air Force and
(despite its limited role at Inchon) its "decisive role"
in the Seoul campaign.

181   Futrell, Robert F.   United States Air Force
Operations in the Korean Conflict, 25 June - 1 November
1950. United States Air Force Historical Division,
Historical Study, Number 71, 1952.

This department of the Air Force book is a limited
introductory account of the role of the United States
Air Force, from the day of America's involvement in
Korea to the end of this period. The air was during the
actual landing, was conducted by naval and marine air
units, but once ashore the Air Force joined the action.
Inchon air defense, from plan to execution, is discussed
in detail. Included are some "air operation" overlays
that spell out different target (as well as command)
areas. Futrell provides the reader with limited but
good coverage.

182 Jackson, Robert. Air War Over Korea. New York:
Scribners, 1973. 175 pages, illustrations, maps,
appendix, bibliography.

A good initial history of the role of air power in
the opening days of the Korean War. Well defined, if
essentially broad, coverage of the air war which was so
essential to delaying first the North Koreans, and then
the Chinese as they pushed the United Nations forces to
the South. Chapter 4 discusses the air aspects of the
Inchon landing, which were limited to Navy and Marine
craft, and move to Seoul, during which all air arms were
utilized.

183 Office of Air Force History. Air Interdiction in
World War II, Korea, and Vietnam; Interviews with Gen.
Earle E. Partridge, General Jacob E. Smart, and General
John W. Vogt, Jr.. Richard H. Kohn and Joseph P.
Harahan. (editors). USAF Warrior Series Government
Printing Office: Office of Air Force History, 1986. 105
pages, index, illustrations, maps.

An interesting look at the poor combat conditions
and command structures between the various services;
all of which led to a lack of idea interdiction. Much
of the problem lay with different methods of calling and
regulating ground-air support, as well as the poor
coordination between units. Contains some brief
comments about Inchon.

184   Office of Air Force History.   _Air Superiority in World War II and Korea: An Interview with Gen. James Ferguson, Gen. Robert M. Lee, Gen. William Momyer, and Lt. General Elwood R. Quesada._   Richard H. Kohn and Joseph P. Harahan. (editors).   USAF Warrior Series Government Printing Office: Office of Air Force History, 1983.   116 pages, index, illustrations, maps, notes, appendix.

Good discussion of X Corps brief control of, and desire to keep operational control of the Marine Air Wing. The agreement imposed by MacArthur ran counter to the air coordination agreement between Army and Air Force which made the senior Air Force general the coordinator of air operations in the Korean theatre. Considerable effort was expended to acquaint area and service contact over aircraft.   The appendix outlines air command and employment of air power.

185   Office of Air Force History.   _Strategic Air Warfare: Interviews with Generals Curtis E. LeMay, Leon W. Johnson, David A. Burchinal, and Jack J. Catton._   Richard H. Kohn and Joseph P. Harahan. (editors).   USAF Warrior Series   Government Printing Office: Office of Air Force History, 1988.

Primarily concerned with the Strategic Air Command, but deals with members and units of that command which appeared in Korea (86 - 90), and the effect of their role near Inchon.   A great deal of the recorded discussions are concerned with command, and ground-air support.

186   Winnefeld, James A. and Dana J. Johnson.   _Joint Air Operations: Pursuit of Unity in Command and Control, 1942-1991._   Annapolis, Maryland: Naval Institute Press, 1993.   219 pages, index, illustrations.

An excellent study of the failure of command between services.   The command question grew to dangerous dimensions especially at this time when pre-war battles were still remembered.   A large section deals with the problems in the Korean War, and in Inchon which was a good example of the compromise of strength and effectiveness that occurred when responsibility and authority was divided.   39 - 60.

ARTICLES

187 "The Air-Ground Operation in Korea" <u>Air Force</u> 34
(1951) 19 - 58.
     The main part of this issue is devoted to a lengthy
consideration of the role played by the Air Force in
flying the ground support missions during the first six
months of the Korean War, but the article fails to
discuss the fact that, because of command difficulties,
it was necessary to remove the Air Force from the Inchon
plan.

188   Dockery, Charles L.   "Marine Air Over Korea"
<u>Marine Corps Gazette</u> 69:12 (December 1985) 38 - 50.
Photos.
     The Marine Aircraft Wing flew combat missions in
support of ground troops both during the landing and
during the push on Seoul. The account covers the Marine
air wing in general but good account of their role at
Inchon and Seoul.

189 Futrell, Robert F. and Albert F. Simpson. "Air War
in Korea" <u>Air University Quarterly Review</u> 4:2 (Fall
1950) 18 - 39; 4:3 (Spring 1951) 47 - 72; 4:4
(Summer 1951) 83 - 89.
     Concerned initial reaction of the Far East Air
Force which was, by Japanese law, only a defense force.
Now they became aggressive. Considers the invasion, use
of air to support ground troops, and strategic bombing.
This account of early air support in Korea includes some
information on the Inchon landing. Material reappears
in his longer history.

190 Guisti, Ernest H. and Kenneth W. Condit. "Marine
Air Over Inchon - Seoul" <u>Marine Corps Gazette</u> 36
(June 1952) 18 - 27.
     During the Inchon-Seoul operation five squadrons
were in action for 18 days with 32 combat sorties
averaged each day per squadron. The loss of eleven
planes, six pilots and one air crewman was remarkably
low given the high degree of close ground support the
planes provided.

191   Kropf, Roger F.   "The US Air Force in Korea: Problems that Hindered the Effectiveness of Air Power" Airpower Journal 4:1 (Spring 1990) 30 - 46.
    A rather ambitious attempt to deal with the problems which seemed to hinder a greater success for the Air Force in the Korean War. The author identifies the problems as poorly selected air bases, difficulty of the joint command structure, and poor air-to-ground coordination. Kropf does not take on the question of why the Air Force was only limitedly involved at the Inchon landing.

192   "United States Air Force Operation in the Korean Conflict, 25 June-1 November 1950" Operational Research Office. United States Air Force Historical Study, Number 71. (July 1952) 44.
    A restricted monograph written to show the extent and success of the Air Force. While overly optimistic, it makes a good case. It was expanded and later published in book form by Robert Futrell. See entry number 180.

193   United States Secretary of Defense. "Air War in Korea" Air University Quarterly Review 4 (1950) 19 -39.
    An official assessment of United States Air Force operations in Korea, 25 June to 1 November 1950. The not too surprising conclusion is that the Air Force did well. Despite the somewhat self-serving attitude this is an excellent source for statistics on sorties flown, targets, when delivered, and how they related to the ground war. The lack of the Air Force at Inchon means this covers the Air Force involvement at the Inchon-Seoul campaign.

194   Weyland, O. P.   "The Air Campaign in Korea" Air University Quarterly Review 6:3 (Fall 1953) 3 - 28.
    This brief account presents an overly optimistic view of the success of both air-to-ground support and strategic bombing. A major problem was that North Korea targets did not present themselves in a manner that allowed the Air Force the full use of its bombing power. Air-to-ground support was not as successful, especially at the beginning, because of command limitations.

Navy

BOOKS

195 Blassingame, Wyatt. <u>The U. S. Frogmen of World War
II</u>. New York: Random House, Landmark Books, 1964. 171
pages, illustrations, maps.
      This is a book for juniors, and less than detailed,
but it is one of the few which deal with the Underwater
Demolition Teams in Korea. Includes list of personnel
who were involved in the early mine-clearing activities.

196 Cagle, Malcolm W. and Frank A. Manson. <u>The Sea War
in Korea</u>. Annapolis, Maryland: Naval Institute, 1967.
555 pages, index, illustrations, appendix.
      The naval war in Korea is excellently covered.
Inchon was a major event for the navy and an account of
the amphibious effort is considered in detail (chapter
11), as is the naval role in bombardment. A significant
part in the MacArthur plan was the North Korean's
overwhelming "preoccupation with defense of his
coastline." The fear created by the Inchon landing had
far-reaching implications.

197 Fane, Francis D. and Don Moore. <u>The Naked Warriors</u>.
New York: Appleton-Century-Crofts, Inc., 1956.   230
pages, index, illustrations.
      A brief personalized history of the Underwater
Demolition Teams operating during World War II and
Korea. A chapter deals with the Korean period of these
unusual underwater warriors who were widely involved at
Inchon prior to, and during, the landing.

198   Field, James A., Jr.   <u>History of United States
Naval Operations: Korea</u>. Washington, DC: Government
Printing Office, 1962. 499 pages, index, maps, charts.
      Certainly one of the better works on the naval
aspects of the Korean War. An excellent account of the
significant role played by the navy in the Inchon
landing, from the sea bombardment of shore
installations, air wing targets, the transport of
troops, to the defense of the exposed troops.
Particularly pages 170 - 218.

199   Hallion, Richard P.   <u>The Naval Air War in Korea</u>.
Baltimore: The Nautical and Aviation Publishing Company
of America, 1986.   244 pages, index, illustrations,
maps.
    Very interesting account of the naval air war.   In
particular, this work deals with the complicated air
support system supplied by the navy before, during, and
after the Inchon landing.   57 - 88.

200   Hoyt, Edwin P.   <u>Carrier Wars</u>.   New York: McGraw-
Hill Publishing, 1989.   274 pages, index, bibliography.
    The Navy had three fast carriers and two escort
carriers as a part of the Inchon landing and air cover.
Hoyt, a prolific and able historian discusses the Korean
War in chapter 19 giving few details but a good overview
of the place of carrier action at Inchon.

201   Isenberg, Michael T.   <u>Shield of the Republic: The
United States Navy in an Era of Cold War and Violent
Peace</u>.   Volume 1, 1945-1962.   New York: St. Martin's
Press, 1993.   948 pages, index, illustrations, maps.
    Very interesting, if strongly opinionated, general
history of the United States Navy with good coverage of
the Korean War, including Inchon.

202   Kelly, Orr.   <u>Brave Men, Dark Waters: The Untold
Story of the Navy SEALS</u>.   Novato, California: Presidio
Press, 1992.   288 pages, index, illustrations.
    Chapter 5 deals with Underwater Demolition Teams
(the pre-SEAL designation) in Korea and with their
efforts at and for the Inchon landing.   A heavily
personalized account of a small and unique force which,
other than Inchon, served primarily as reconnaissance
and interdiction forces.   Three UDT groups were
available during the war, only one was utilized at
Inchon.

203   <u>Korean Cruise USS St. Paul CA 73</u>.   Berkeley,
California: Lederer, 1951.
    The account of the <u>USS St. Paul</u>, one of the first
heavy cruisers to arrive in Korean waters, 12 August
1950, in support of ground troops.   It continued on
station until 21 May 1951.

204   The Korean Cruise of the USS Tingey DD 539. San
Diego, California: Davidson, 1951.
    Narrative of the contribution made by an American
destroyer in the early days of the Korean War. These
"greyhounds of the sea" were, as usual, right in the
heart of everything, especially at Inchon and provided
bombardments, escort, and supply missions.

205 Lansdown, John. With the Carriers in Korea: The
Fleet   Air   Arm   Story.   Worcester: Square   One
Publications, 1992.   485 pages, index, illustrations,
maps.
    A long awaited and much heralded study of the use
of carriers in Korea, and their role in the air war.
British in approach and concern but of value for any
look at the Inchon landing.

206 Lott, Arnold S. Most Dangerous Sea. Annapolis,
Maryland: United States Naval Institute, 1959.   322
pages, index, illustrations, maps.
    A personal, and interesting, history of the United
States Navy anti-mine warfare. In chapter 16, "A Few
Minesweepers," Lott tells the story of the Korean
campaign, including Inchon, and the effort of the
understrength minesweepers to clear and keep clear, the
harbors of Korea.

207   One Year of Naval Operations in Korea.   No
publisher, 1951. Annapolis, Maryland: Nimitz Library,
bound typescript.   20 pages.
    The USS Juneau fired the opening salvo of the war
which, for the Navy, eventually expended more than 70
million pounds of high explosives in support of troops.
The first year of the war, including Inchon, is
carefully chronicled.

208   Potter. E. B.   The Naval Academy Illustrated
History of the United States Navy. New York: Galahad
Books, 1971. 299 pages, maps, diagrams, illustrations.
    A very common book which is included here only
because of the excellent sea map and description of the
navy role during the Inchon landing. A role which is
poorly covered in general.

209 Schratz, Paul R. <u>Submarine Commander: A Story of World War II and Korea</u>. Lexington, Kentucky: The University Press of Kentucky, 1988. 322 pages, index, illustrations.

While generally an account of the exploits of Captain Schratz during two wars, not unlike many that are available, it does introduce the interesting fact of submarine use in a ground war. The <u>USS Pickerel</u> was involved in some briefly related activities, but he comments on the activities of other subs which were more directly involved with diversionary tactics, surveys, and secret landings.

210 Sheldon, Walt. <u>Hell or High Water: MacArthur's Landing at Inchon</u>. New York: The Macmillan Company, 1968. 340 pages, maps, illustrations.

An excellent and detailed study of the Inchon landing from conception to the wrap-up. The success was the result of MacArthur's determination. Never the secret it was claimed (called "Operation Common Knowledge" by many of the press) it was the result of one man's determination. Despite the opposition of President, Pentagon, typhoons, and high water the carefully planned attack was all MacArthur promised it would be.

211 Smith, M. S. <u>The Korea Cruise USS Philippine Sea CV-47</u>. Berkeley, California: Lederer, 1951.

From July 1950 to June 1951 the <u>USS Philippine Sea</u> was one of the carriers operating off the coast, sailing in support of the ground troops and taking part in the Inchon landing.

ARTICLES

212 "British Commonwealth Naval Operations During the Korean War" <u>Royal United Service Institution Journal</u> I 96 (May 1951) 250 - 255; II 96 (November 1951) 609 -616; III 97 (May 1952) 241 - 248.

This article traces the efforts of the Commonwealth naval forces during the Korean Conflict, including in part I, which include those involved in the Inchon landing.

213 Cagle, Malcolm W. "Carrier Jets Over Korea" Skyways 10:7 (July 1951) 10 - 12, 57.
A brief popularized version of his excellent longer and more serious work, with Frank A. Manson on the naval war in Korea.

214 Denson, John. "Captain Thach's Phantom Carrier" Collier's 126 (October 14, 1950) 18 - 19, 52 - 56.
Describes the operations of the escort carrier (CVE) USS Sicily and its destroyer escort, USS James E. Kyes and USS Doyle which formed a task group designed to harass the enemy's east coast, striking with phantom like characteristics.

215 Griffin, Harry K. "The Navy in Korean Waters" Army Information Digest 6:12 (December 1951) 12 - 22.
A brief but inclusive account of the navy during the first year of the war. Griffin points out that the navy was heavily involved in the war from the very beginning, offering support both in terms of firepower on selected targets and logistical support to the ground troops. This work includes material on amphibious supply, off-shore bombardment, and minesweeping all of which took place in conjunction with the landing at Inchon.

216 Hittle, J. D. "Korea: Back to the Facts of Life" United States Naval Institute Proceedings 76:12 (December 1950) 1289 - 1298.
The author is concerned with protecting the "balanced fleet concept" and uses the successful attack on Inchon as an example of the cooperation between the Marines and the United States Navy.

217 Holly, David C. "The ROK Navy: Reorganization After World War II with US Aid; Its Record During the Korean Conflict" United States Naval Institute Proceedings 78:11 (November 1952) 1218 - 1225.
Two United States destroyers were recommissioned in the ROK navy, the first in 375 years, as the United States developed a naval force for South Korea. While small and primarily US trained and equipped, the ROK navy did play an important role at the Inchon landing.

218 Horan, H. E. "British Aircraft Carriers in Korean Waters" Royal Air Force Quarterly 5 (April 1953) 133 - 138.

The British carriers provided the "depth" for United Nations actions, as well as the planes used for deception and interdiction during the early phase.

219 Karig, Walter, Malcolm W. Cagle, and Frank A. Manson. "The Man Who Made Inchon Possible" 202 - 213. Donald B. Robinson The Dirty Wars: Guerrilla Actions and Other Forms of Unconventional Warfare. New York: Delacorte Press, 1968. 356 pages, index.

An eye-witness account of Lieutenant Eugene Franklin Clark, United States Navy who, with a corp of South Korean youth, lived behind enemy lines at Inchon to map items of land, tides, weather, and enemy positions to make possible the landing at Inchon. Informative account of preparations for the landing.

220 Keighley, Larry. "Four Dead -- Three Wounded" Saturday Evening Post 223:17 (October 21, 1950) 32 - 33, 157.

Account of LCVP (Landing Craft, Vehicle and Personnel) Number 8 during the attack on Red Beach at Inchon. In this first time landing against a large city, four were killed and three hit in the first minutes.

221 Kim, Sang Mo. "The Implications of the Sea War in Korea" Naval War College Review 20 (Summer 1967) 105 - 139.

A South Korean naval officer discusses the lessons learned during the war, including the significance of amphibious operations.

222 Knight, Charlotte. "Men of the Mine Sweepers" Collier's 128:19 (November 10, 1951) 13 - 15, 66 - 68.

Account of the mine sweepers which were responsible for clearing the harbors off the coast of Korea. Basically a high-risk "one-on-one" exercise. Seems to be more an acknowledgement of their high percentage of naval casualties.

223   Lovell, Kenneth C.   "Navy Engineer Support in Korea" <u>Military Engineer</u> 44 (November-December 1952) 413 - 417.
    A rare account of the significant actions of the 104th Naval Construction Battalion (Seabees) who were in direct support during the Inchon landing.

224   McMullen, Robert A. and Nicholas A. Canzona. "Wolmi-do: Turning the Key" <u>United States Naval Institute Proceedings</u> 82:3 (March 1956) 290 - 297.
    Up until 10 September, 1950, the North Koreans were having a pretty good war. Then the bombardment of Wolmi-do began. Indepth account of the planning for, and execution of, the taking of Wolmi-do, the island which was the necessary first step in the landing.

225   Meacham, James.   "Four Mining Campaigns: An Historical Analysis of the Decisions of the Commanders" <u>Naval War College Review</u> 19 (June 1967) 75 - 129.
    Looks at and compares the effects of four mining campaigns, then provides an analysis of the wisdom of the commanders involved in handling the situation. In the process he provides a good look a the Inchon versus Wonsan mine situation and the lack of preparation on the side of the United States.

226   Montross, Lynn and Nicholas A. Canzona.   "Large Sedentary Targets on Red Beach" <u>Marine Corps Gazette</u> 44:9 (September 1960) 44 - 50.
    Part of the "audacious gamble" at Inchon was the beaching of 8 LST's (Landing Ship Tanks) at H hour plus 1 hour. In this way much needed supplies were available for landing -- tanks, rations, gas, ammo, water -- as well as providing four surgical teams for immediate medical care. The officers and crews are listed.

227   Scott-Moncrieff, A. K.   "Navy Operations in Korean Waters" <u>Royal United Service Institution Journal</u> 98 (May 1953) 218 - 227.
    Excellent account of Commonwealth involvement, associated with the United Nations command an Inchon, and beyond. The British response was very timely and significant.

228   "Three Very Long Minutes"   <u>United States Naval</u>
<u>Institute Proceedings</u> 76:12 (December 1950) 1365 -
1369.
       A photographic essay of naval aircraft from Task
Force 77 in support of the Inchon landing. One of the
results of the naval aspect of the Korean War was a
renewal of understanding the value of the aircraft
carrier in support of land operations. Deals with
aircraft at Inchon and includes one of the first photos
of a helicopter air-sea rescue.

229   Wheeler, Gerald.   "Naval Aviation in the Korean
War" <u>United States Naval Institute Proceedings</u> 83:7
(July 1957) 767 - 777.
       There is no substitute for control of the sea and
the sky, and fairly quickly, this was accomplished. But
if there is no strong air support of troops this is not
fully effective. Wheeler discusses the way in which
naval-ground support was a major contribution to that
control.

230   Worden, William L. "The Trick That Won Seoul"
<u>Saturday Evening Post</u> 223:20 (November 11, 1950) 22.
       The <u>USS Collett</u> (DD 730) joined five other
destroyers during the invasion of Wolmi-do Island, drew
fire and baited the enemy to test the strength of the
forces facing the Marines who were to land, then
supported with ground support fire.

The Seoul Phase of the Campaign

BOOK

231   Military History Section.   <u>The First Ten Years: A</u>
<u>Short History of the Eighth United States Army, 1944 -</u>
<u>1954</u>.   Eighth U. S. Army, n.d.   41 pages, index,
illustrations, maps.
       Brief history with simple, but excellent, maps
which traces the role of the Eighth Army.   Clear
description of Eighth Army response to Inchon landing
(19 - 20) and the move toward Seoul.

ARTICLES

232   Alsop, Joseph.   "Matter of Fact"   Leatherneck
33:12 (1950) 33.
    An accurate and interesting account of the Inchon
to Seoul campaign by Alsop, a well know newspaper man
who was covering Korea.

233 Canzona, Nicholas. "Dog Company's Charge" United
States Naval Institute Proceedings 82:7 (July 1956)
1203 - 1212.
    An account of Company D, 2nd Battalion, 5th
Regiment and the taking of Seoul following the Inchon
invasion.   The action, led by a rifle company, showed
that five years into the atomic age, the work of
clearing a city was still to be done by rifle squads.
A point by point account of the action.

234 "The Fall of Seoul: US Marines in Street Fighting
Proceeding September 28" London News 217 (October 7,
1950) 556-557.
    Focuses on the house-to-house nature of the Seoul
phase of the campaign.   This sort of fighting was a new
form for the Marines, and required some adaptation of
procedures.

235 Klimp, Jack L.   "The Battle for Seoul: Marines and
MOUT" Marine Corps Gazette 65 (November 1981) 79 -
82.
    Discusses the use of the "Military Operations on
Urbanized Terrain" outfit.   The urban fight was not the
same as the open beach and jungle they had trained for.
This is a discussion of the defeat of Seoul which makes
the case for mechanized units within the Marines.

236 Montross, Lynn.   "The Capture of Seoul - Battle of
the Barricades" Marine Corps Gazette 35:8 (August
1951) 26 - 37.
    A continuation of Montross' excellent accounts of
the Inchon landing and the battle for Seoul.   In this
segment he deals with the assault by Marine infantry,
the crossing of the Han, and the final assault on Seoul.
Supported by excellent maps.

237 Stanford, N. R. "Road Junction" <u>Marine Corps Gazette</u> 35:9 (September 1951) 16 - 21.
     At the crossing of the Han, and in the middle of Seoul, a rifle company commander discovers that there are times when you have to throw away the book. This article is a vivid account of small unit action and tense command decisions during the battle for Seoul.

238 Tallent, Robert W. "Inchon to Seoul" <u>Leatherneck</u> 34:1 (1951) 12 - 17.
     An enlisted man's account of the drive from Inchon to Seoul which, at least from his perspective, was not the easy task sometimes described.

239 Tallent, Robert W. "Street Fight in Seoul" Karl Schuon. (editor). <u>The Leatherneck: An Informal History of the U. S. Marines</u>. New York: Franklin Watts, Inc., 1993. 240 - 249.
     The 7th Regiment, 1st Marine Division, missed the landing but the unit arrived from the United States in time to participate in the advance against Seoul. This is an excellent account of urban warfare, a somewhat unusual fighting arena for the marines.

Evaluation and Analysis

BOOKS

240 Bailey, Sydney D. <u>The Korean Armistice</u>. New York: St Martin's Press, 1992. 312 pages, maps.
     This study is about the convoluted processes by which the Korean War ended short of victory. It takes a very detailed look at the fighting of the war as each action, advance and retreat, was measured against the undecided factor of victory or negotiation. Strong background (20 - 27) of the reasoning and impact of Inchon. Excellent source of Security Council Resolutions, principal documents of the negotiations, and an interesting collection (throughout) of MacArthur excuses.

241 Crowe, Clarance. <u>An Analysis of the Inchon-Seoul Campaign</u>. Maxwell Air Force Base, Alabama, March 1983. Research Report for Air Command and Staff College, 90 pages.

   This is an evaluation of the military effort, and achievement, from the point of view of command. It is the product of students at the command classes of the Air Command and Staff College. It is located at the University library. It is not classified, but unavailable to the scholar, unless they receive special permission from the staff at the college.

242 Donovan, Robert J. <u>Nemesis: Truman and Johnson in the Coils of War in Asia</u>. New York: St. Martin's Press, 1984. 216 pages, index.

   Excellent study of the crisis of the Asian wars as experienced by presidents Truman and Johnson. Considers the Inchon landing as a part of the overall political implications of the whole Korean question, which lured the presidents into the belief that victory was possible. 83 - 88, 124.

243 Goncharov, Sergei N., John W. Lewis, and Xue Litai. <u>Uncertain Partners: Stalin, Mao, and the Korean War</u>. Stanford, California: Stanford University Press, 1993. 450 pages, index.

   An essential, and scholarly, work which provides new and important information. Based on primary source materials, most of which has just recently become available, which shows the support, albeit reluctantly, of Stalin and Mao for the North Korean invasion against the South. Mao's decision to intervene in the North was made weeks before the Inchon landing, thus changing many of the theories concerning North Korean reaction to the landing.

244 Hampson, Gary. <u>Strategic Sealift Lessons Learned: A Historical Perspective</u>. Fort McNair, DC: Industrial College of the Armed Forces, Executive Research Project, 1988. 26 pages.

   An excellent analysis of the size and effectiveness of the logistical problem involved in fighting a war 4000 miles form the resources.

245   Heller, Francis H.   The Korean War: A 25 Year
Perspective.   Lawrence, Kansas: The Regents Press of
Kansas, 1977.   251 pages, index, illustrations.
    This 25-year look at the Korean War contains some
very interesting information, but the most significant
is the early discussion of the war by a panel of
participants. One of the topics is Inchon, during which
General Matthew B. Ridgway made some insightful
comments.

246   Khong, Yuen Foong.   Analogies at War: Korea,
Munich, Dien Bien Phu, and the Vietnam Decisions of
1965.   Princeton, New Jersey: Princeton University
Press, 1992.   286 pages, index.
    Another attempt to place the Korean War within the
larger context of the Cold War, all of which led to
American involvement in Vietnam. His position, that
what the United States thought they had learned in Korea
[including those learned from the Inchon experience]
explains why the Johnson administration felt it
necessary to be involved in Vietnam.

247   Lee, Chae-Jin. (editor).   The Korean War: 40 Year
Perspective. Claremont McKenna College: Keck Center for
International and Strategic Studies. Monograph Number 1,
1991.   131 pages.
    This is very difficult to locate. It is the first
of the Center's monographs dealing with the Korean War.
This perspective looks at the war from the both
political and military points of view now, nearly half-
a-century after the armistice was signed.

248   Mayers, David A.   Cracking the Monolith: U.S.
Policy Against the Sino-Soviet Alliance, 1949-1955.
Baton Rouge: Louisiana State University Press, 1986.
176 pages, index.
    A wide look at the long range diplomatic plan to
divide the unity of the communist block. Of interest
here only in its interpretations of the landing and
victory at Inchon. The assumption of victory, and the
opportunity to cross the parallel, is seen in the light
of America's "classical diplomacy," i.e. to somehow
drive a wedge between China and Russia.

249   Mueller, John E.   <u>War, Presidents and Public Opinion</u>. New York: John Wiley & Sons, Inc., 1973.   300 pages, index, charts, graphs.
    A highly readable discussion of the popularity of both the Korean War and the Vietnam War.   Contains several surveys dealing with period response to the war, and a chapter dealing with retrospective support.

250   Poats, Rutherford.   <u>Decision in Korea</u>. New York: The McBride Company, 1954.   340 pages, index, maps.
    Poats' point is that the war was not fought to win, but rather to show Russia the American determination to support any country against communist aggression.   The Inchon movement, referred to in his chapter as the "Hammer and Anvil," was designed to show American military determination, but it was an awesome risk that could have been avoided.

251   Ryan, Mark A.   <u>Chinese Attitudes Toward Nuclear Weapons: China and the United States During the Korean War</u>.   London, England: An East Gate Book, 1989.   325 pages, index.
    The title is somewhat misleading.   It is about the willingness to go to war even in the shadow of nuclear weapons.   The early phases of the book deal with the War, including Inchon, and the misunderstandings (thus probably lack of fear) concerning the power of the bomb.

ARTICLES

252   Blumenson, Martin.   "MacArthur's Divided Command: An Assessment in the Light of Army Doctrine"   <u>Army</u>   7 (November 1956) 38 - 44.
    By dividing command MacArthur violated a principle of war long followed.   Divided command accomplished the mission at Inchon, but was it successful overall?   It was done because of the communication problems caused by the Taebaek Mountains which would separate the command, and the general problem of communication.   Yet as the United Nations troops moved North each appeared ignorant of the other.   The decision, however important to MacArthur, caused trouble for Walker at Pusan, and a later disharmony in command.

253   Cagle, Malcolm W.   "Errors of the Korean War"
United States Naval Institute Proceedings 84:1 (March
1958) 31 - 35.
       After accepting Inchon as a valid effort, this Navy
historian identified several errors; 1) the decision to
land at Wonsan   2) retreating too far after China
entered the war   3) the failure to coordinate aerial
interdiction at the theatre level, and 4) failure to
adopt the Navy "close air support system."   But the
greatest failure overall was timidity, the unwillingness
to win.

254   Cagle, Malcolm W.   "Inchon: The Analysis of a
Gamble" United States Naval Institute Proceedings 80:1
(January 1954) 47 - 51.
       The chances of a military disaster were great.
Three problems existed: physical (terrain); military
handicap (removal of troops from Pusan at the most
dangerous time); and the political effects on China who
were willing to allow a compromise but not an essential
United Nations victory.   The odds were 5000 to 1 and
those are too large.

255   Cottrell, Alvin J. and James E. Dougherty.   "The
Lessons of Korea: War and the Power of Man" Orbis 2
(Spring 1958) 39 - 64.
       An interesting account of the impact of limited
war, and the failure of the United States to see the
Korean Conflict in light of its strategic background.
The United States never fully understood the
relationship between military success and political
movement in Korea.

256   "The Defeat of the American Eighth Army in Korea,
November - December, 1950" 165 - 196 Eliot A. Cohen
and John Gooch. Military Misfortunes: The Anatomy of
Failure in War. New York: The Free Press, 1990. 296
pages, index.
       While actually addressing the military failure at
Chosin, it takes a look at the significant phase of the
war, Inchon, which they call the "aggregate failure."
All this begins with the landing and assumptions of
Inchon which scared the Chinese into action.

257 Falk, Stanley L. "Comments on Reynolds: 'MacArthur as Maritime Strategist'" Naval War College Review 33 (March/April 1980) 92 - 99.
      The author attacks Clark G. Reynolds who called MacArthur a great maritime strategist. According to Falk's well presented argument MacArthur's planning was limited and outdated. The General failed to appreciate the logistical aspects of naval operations. Highly critical of the Inchon landing.

258 Folson, S. B. "Korea -- A Reflection From the Air" United States Naval Institute Proceedings 82:7 (July 1956) 733 - 735.
      Folson contends that the situation was such that the United Nations could not claim to have total air superiority, primarily because of the North Korean ability to move supplies at night. The United Nations inability to hit the enemy, meant that the job could not be accomplished.   In a very real sense, the effectiveness of the air war was reduced because of lack of targets.

259   Hamby, Alonzo L.   "Public Opinion: Korea and Vietnam" Wilson Quarterly 2 (Summer 1978).
      Hamby asserts a comparison between the American attitude toward the Asian wars in Korea and Vietnam. What they discovered was that the early protests against the Korean War came from the political Right.   The protestors used and honored the American flag in their protests.

260 Hunt, Michael H.   "Beijing and the Korean Crisis, June 1950 - June 1951" Political Science Quarterly 107:3 (1992) 453 - 478.
      Hunt's work reflects the increasing availability of Soviet and Chinese documents relating to the North Korean decision to invade and the Chinese decision to intervene.   Of significance here is that the Inchon landing is seen as a vital factor in the Chinese involvement, for it both suggested an American threat to Chinese security, but was also seen as a major boost to the cause of the counterrevolutionaries in China, and thus required a strong government reaction.

261 "The Inchon Landings" <u>The American Legion</u> (July 1993) 24 - 27, 61.
A brief but informed account of the landing at Inchon which showed that the amphibious assault is "the most powerful tool we have." Describes the attack as so successful, so well planned, and accomplished so quickly that casualties were surprisingly low.

262 McLellan, David S. "Dean Acheson and the Korean War" <u>Political Science Quarterly</u> 83 (1968) 16 - 39.
Determines that Acheson miscalculated China's intentions in Korea, thus Truman acted with less than a realistic assessment in 1950.

263 "President" <u>Department of State Bulletin</u> 23 (October 9, 1950) 586.
The text of President Harry Truman's message of congratulations to MacArthur on the Inchon success, and General MacArthur's reply to the President.

264 Reynolds, Clark G.   "MacArthur as Maritime Strategist" <u>Naval War College Review</u> 33 (March/April 1980) 79 - 91.
The author develops great praise for the Maritime strategies (the combined use of Navy, Army, Air Force in a seaborne operation) of General MacArthur who developed a strong policy in Korea, especially the Inchon landing. MacArthur had more faith in the Navy, than the Navy did in themselves.

265 Stilwell, Richard. "A Victory Not to Be Forgotten" <u>The American Legion</u> (June 1990) 30, 49 - 50.
Stilwell holds that the Korean War was pivotal in postwar history and politics and thus beneficial to the United States and Allies.   Appears to be overly patriotic.

266 "Turning of the Tide in Korea and the Meeting of 'A New Foe'" <u>United Nations Bulletin</u> 9:10 (1950) 528 - 535.
Includes the official report from Commanding General MacArthur covering the Inchon invasion and the capture of Seoul.

267   Wages, C. J.   "Mines...The Weapons that Wait"
<u>United States Naval Institute Proceedings</u> 88 (May
1962) 103 - 113.
    Naval mines are the ideal weapon for "have-not"
nations. And in the Korean War America lost control of
the seas to a nation without a navy using pre-World War
I weapons. The United Nations were not prepared for the
North Korean and Russian use of mines, and it cost the
United States control of the sea. As well, over the
Inchon period, cost several ships and many lives.

SUPPORT

Media and the Landing

BOOKS

268   Cumings, Bruce.   <u>War and Television</u>.   London:
Verso, 1992.   309 pages, index, illustrations.
    Of the eight chapters Cumings, a respected
historian of the Korean War, uses five to describe the
conflicts that exist between official and unofficial
documentaries, and to describe the difficulty in filming
the story of the Korean War. Not strictly on Inchon,
but on the political problems with reporting the war.
It is part "apology" for the failure of the British
"Korea" film and part analysis of the television
coverage of American wars. Chapters 5, 6, and 7 deal
with television's attempts to bring coverage (historical
and documentary) on the Korean War, but ends up being an
analysis of documentary attempts.

269   Jones, Charles and Eugene.   <u>The Face of War</u>. New
York: Prentice-Hall,   Inc.,   1951.   166   pages,
illustrations.
    A photo essay of the 1st Marine Division at war.
Chapters 5, 6, and 7 deal with the marines during the
battles at Inchon and Seoul.   The essays are very
informative, but the pictures themselves present an
excellent story as well. 66 - 163.

270   Kahn, Ely J.   The Peculiar War: Impressions of a
Reporter in Korea.   New York: Random House, 1952.   211
pages.
        Kahn considers the nature of the Korean War, and
also gives a lot of attention to the early military
leaders, their prejudices and failures, as well as the
successes.

271 King, O. H. P. Tail of the Paper Tiger. Caldwell,
Idaho: The Caxton Printers, Ltd., 1961.   574 pages,
index.
        A highly critical account of the war by
participant, Associated Press reporter O. H. P. King, of
a war that "was never meant to be won."   Primarily a
chronological report with the Inchon landing discussed
specifically 113, 239 - 240, 384 - 390, 430, 435.

272 Moeller, Susan D.   Shooting War: Photography and
the American Combat Experience. New York: Basic Books,
1991.   474 pages, index, illustrations.
        Part four "The Korean War" (251 - 324) deals with
the role of, and use of, combat photography during the
Korean Conflict, including coverage of the Inchon
landing. Asserts photojournalists were less restricted
than other correspondents.

ARTICLES

273   "Battle of Korea: Over the Beaches"   Time   56
(September 25, 1950) 25 - 31.
        An indepth reporting of the Inchon landing with
selected coverage of MacArthur and the naval officers
responsible for landing the troops. Reminds the reader
of World War II island hopping coverage, but does
provide some interesting information about the landing.

274   Dorn, Frank.   "Briefing the Press"   Army
Information Digest 6 (1951) 36 - 41.
        Describes the procedure by which the Department of
Defense disseminated news to the press during the first
six months. The news that was released rarely told the
American people what was happening, and was especially
quiet about the difficulties involved.

275 Erwin, Ray. "Censorship, Communications Worry 200 K-War Correspondence" <u>Education Public</u> 83 (1950) 7, 44.
      Erwin discusses the problems of war correspondents during the early weeks of the war. Rules of reporting constantly changed depending on what military jurisdiction was calling the shots. The confusion was not simply policy but reflected a growing anger at what the military considered to be "unwise" reporting. This article's value is that it includes the names of most correspondents on the scene at the time.

276 Fleming, Kenneth. "Hell Run Over Korea" <u>Leatherneck</u> 33 (1950) 18 - 20.
      Discusses the difficulty for carrier-based air photographers who risked life and limb to eventually provide clear pictures of United Nations military movement.

277   Kaff, Al.   "War Correspondents Revisit Korean Battlefields" <u>Editor & Publisher</u> 123:28 (July 14, 1990) 30.
      An interesting account of early correspondents during the war, including Bill Shinn's story of the Inchon landing before the operation was announced. All in all more that 350 correspondents were accredited to the United Nations command and 18 were killed.

278 Lee, Raymond S. H.   "Early Korean War Coverage" <u>Journalism Quarterly</u> 55 (1978) 789 - 792.
      Reviewing four South Korean papers, and three large American papers, the author suggests that American papers were more accurate than Korean ones.

279   Walker, Hank and Carl Mydans. (photographer, editor).   "The Invasion: The Pattern of the War is Changed As U. N. Forces Strike the Red Rear" <u>Life</u> 29:14 (October 2, 1950) 23 - 32.
      A photo essay of the invasion which contains a good "I was there" report on the landing. The wide angle picture of the landing beaches is worth ten maps in understanding the landing difficulties. The essay covers through the fall of Kimpo airfield and the attack on Seoul.

Intelligence

ARTICLE

280 DeWeerd, Harvey A.   "Strategic Surprise in the Korean War" Orbis 6:3 (Fall 1963) 435 - 452.
    While directed to the Korean War in general it does deal with the "mishandling of strategic intelligence" and tries to explain why the United States was so unprepared. What is not discussed, and should be in such a work, is the American failure to keep its own activities secret. The surprise is that the United States managed to keep any secrets at all. The Inchon landing was well known long before it was executed.

Logistics, Support, and Leadership

BOOKS

281 Cowdery, Albert E.   United States Army in the Korean War: The Medic's War. Washington, DC: Office of Military History, 1987.   391 pages, index, illustrations, maps.
    Chapter 4 "The Medical Service in the Attack" deals with medical services provided for the landing forces, preparations for which were complicated by the speed of the program, and the foul weather they encountered. During this period "the medical services underwent a radically compressed and intensive learning experience."

282 Dunstan, Simon.   Armour of the Korean War 1950-1953. London: Osprey Publishing, 1982.   41 pages, illustrations.
    Brief illustrated history of the heavy armor used by both the United States and the North Korean (Soviet) during the war. The static nature of the war, toward the end, limited tanks but it was such armor that moved the North Koreans rapidly south. Illustrations are excellent.

283   Martin, John G.   It Began at Imphal: The Combat
Cargo Story.   Manhattan, Kansas: Sunflower University
Press, 1988.   98 pages, index, illustrations, maps.
    An interesting and informative account of a little
known aspect of warfare.   It traces the air combat cargo
aspect of fighting in World War II and Korea (73 - 90).
The whole nature of air cargo is very relevant to the
landing, and the work includes the account of an
emergency delivery of a pontoon bridge, left behind by
mistake and, needed in the advance from Inchon.

284   Mesko, Jim.   Armor in Korea.   Squadron/Signal
Publications, 1983.   80 pages, illustrations.
    Illustration of armor during the landing,
considerable detailed drawings and discussion of early
availability and use.

285   Reister, Frank.   Battle Casualties and Medical
Statistics: U. S. Army Experience in the Korean War.
Washington, DC: The Surgeon General, 1973.   173 pages,
charts.
    An action by action listing of battle casualties as
well as supporting medical statistics for the serious
inquirer.   The Inchon landing period is separated so as
to identify the costs in terms of manpower.

286   Thompson, Annis G.   The Great Airlift: The Story of
Combat Cargo.   Tokyo: Dai-Nippon Printing Company, 1954.
463 pages, 50% illustrations.
    Primarily a report of the role of the 315th Air
Division in supplying the troops early in the war.   A
remarkable achievement well documented.

287   Westover, John G.   Combat Support in Korea.
Washington, DC: Center of Military History, Government
Printing Office, 1987.   254 pages, index, illustrations,
maps.
    This edition of the U. S. Army in Action Series, is
an excellent account of the logistical problems created
by the conflict in Korea, and how the American Army was
able to address them.   This is primarily an oral history
report provided by men on the spot dealing with the
logistical concerns from the opening days of the war.

ARTICLES

288 Banks, Charles L. "Inchon To Seoul: Service In
Action" Marine Corps Gazette 35:5 (May 1951) 20 -
21.
     Supporting and supplying the 1st Marine Division in
its landing at Inchon, and in the eighteen mile drive to
Seoul, created significant problems for the division's
service units.   The speed of assembly and the rapid
movement toward Seoul, made the job even more difficult.
Many new techniques and doctrines were tested in battle
for the first time and found successful.

289 Flanagan, William J. "Korean War Logistics: The
First Hundred Days" Army Logistician 18 (March -
April 1986) 34 - 38.
     The Korean War was one of the best recent examples
of a "come-as-you-are" conventional warfare.   Despite
all the promises of the "atomic" age, this was a war
fought primarily with conventional equipment from
storage.   Flanagan provides fifteen logistical lessons
which must be learned if the United Nations is to meet
further challenges of this nature.

290 Griffin, Harry K. "Typhoon at Kobe" Marine Corps
Gazette 35:9 (September 1951) 60 - 65.
     With the Inchon invasion locked into a September
15, 1950, landing date Lt. Colonel R. L. Blust,
commanding the port of Kobe in southern Japan, was given
the job of loading the troops and their supplies.   Faced
with this task he worked through unbelievable, if
normal, difficulties but had his greatest challenge with
the arrival of typhoon "Jane".   Time was lost and ships
damaged, but they managed to sail on schedule.

291 Hume, Edgar E. "United Nations Medical Service in
the Korean Conflict" Military Surgeon 109 (1951) 91 -
95.
     A look at the United Nations service activities,
including the multi-national force provisions for
medical service.   The need, and initial response, felt
during the first few months of the war is reviewed.

292   Launius, Roger A.   "MATS and the Korean War Airlift" <u>Airlift</u> 12:2 (Summer 1990) 16 - 21.
Brief history by this NASA historian concerning the Military Air Transport System during the early phase of the war, and the prolonged need to move men and equipment in and out of Korea.

293 Mann, Frank L. "Operation 'Versatile'" <u>Military Engineers</u> 44:299 (May-June 1952) 168 - 173.
The 2nd Engineer Special Brigade went ashore with the Marines and were in operation, and by D+1 provided port operation as well as emergency construction.

294 Marsh, Walter. "Army Surgical Hospitals at Work in Korea" <u>Army Information Digest</u> 8 (1953) 48 - 52.
Describes the utilization of Army Surgical Hospitals during the first months of the war when three units were in operation. Medical evacuation was cut considerably by the success of these units.

295   Morgan, Len.   "M*A*S*H Epilogue" <u>Flying</u> 110 (March 1983) 60 - 63.
Using the popular television series as background, the author discusses the early role of the Mobile Medical units, the introduction of the helicopter ambulances, and their success particularly during the early days of the war.

296 "Operation Load-Up" <u>Quartermaster Review</u> 30:3 (1950) 40 - 41, 109 - 110.
A very interesting account of the joint Army, Navy and Marine Corp efforts to load the 1st Marine Division at Kobe Base, Japan. This twelve day ordeal was a major accomplishment not only of supply, but of cooperation.

297   Walker, Stanley L.   "Logistics of the Inchon Landing" <u>Army Logistician</u> (July - August 1981) 34 - 38.
Logistics support planning, preparation, and execution of the 15 September 1950 amphibious landing of the 1st Marine Division at Inchon was accomplished in less than 33 days, including Marine equipment moved from Barstow, California.

OTHER SOURCES

Dissertations and Theses

298 Burk, Richard J. "The Organization and Command of United Nations Military Forces" Master's thesis, Yale University, 1956.
   Traces the difficulties encountered by attempts at a United Nations Command. The early days were fairly simple with only American and ROK troops involved, but as more United Nations forces became involved, the difficulties of language and command increased.

299 CiCola, Louis F. "The Korean War as Seen by the Chicago Tribune, the New York Times, and the Time of London" Thesis, Kent State University, 1981.
   An analysis of war coverage by three major newspapers. They reflect not only national policy but local interests, including critics of Inchon, the war and MacArthur.

300 Johnson, Lisa D. "No Place for a Woman: A Biographical Study of War Correspondent Marguerite Higgins" Master's thesis, East Texas State University, 1983.
   Marguerite Higgins would have disagreed with the author for she felt it was very much her place to be there. This thesis describes Higgins as a very aggressive correspondent during the early phases of the war, where she sent daily dispatches despite the misgivings of the military commanders.

301 Kim, Soon Nam. "The Conduct of The Korean War, 1950-1953: With Emphasis on the Civilian Control over the Military in the United States" University of Aberdeen, 1987. 360 pages, index, bibliography.
   In a very interesting study of civilian control in general the author addressed the role of General Douglas MacArthur. In chapter 4, he deals with the Inchon decision and presents the case that the decision to land troops at Inchon was an example of how MacArthur was able to take preeminence over civilian authority both by the power of his argument and power of this position.

302 Ohm, Chang-Il. "The Joint Chiefs of Staff and U. S.
Policy and Strategy Regarding Korea, 1945-1953" Ph. D.
dissertation, University of Kansas, 1983.
      Ohm holds that the Joint Chiefs of Staff could not
relate what was happening Korea to the larger strategic
interests for America, and thus waffled in their policy
and actions during the War.   Such lack of clarity,
especially in the beginning made the war very costly.

Fiction

BOOKS

303 Axelsson, Arne.   Restrained Response: American
Novels of the Cold War and Korea, 1945 - 1962.   New
York: Greenwood Press, 1990.   221 pages.
      An analysis of Korean War novels, as few as there
are, and dealing with the various phases of the war as
seen in fiction.   Inchon did not emerge as one phase
which appeared in fiction.

304   Joo-Young, Kim.   The Sound of Thunder. Seoul,
Korea: Si-sa-yong-o-sa, Inc. 1990.   325 pages.
      A novel set in the bedlam of the Korean War it is an
example of what has become known as "division-
literature" a genre of novels concerning the division of
Korea and the response to the atrocities of war.   Good
view of the landing from the Korean side.

305 Lloyd, Adrien. Inchon Diary. Wayne, Pennsylvania:
Banbury Books, Inc. 295 pages.
      A worse that usual novel of a woman correspondent
covering the early phases of the Korean War, including
the Inchon period.

306 McCaull, Julian.   The Hinge.   New York: Alcyone
Publication, 1984.   361 pages.
      A fictionalized account of minesweepers and
destroyers, Aware, Award, and Merritt at work on mines
at Wonsan.

307   Packwood, Norval E. Jr.   Leatherhead in Korea.
Quantico, Virginia: Marine Corps Gazette, 1952.   79
pages.
    A cartoon look at the 1st Marine Division from
reorganization and staffing by reserves through the
fight at Inchon and Seoul. This is a strong editorial
piece which gives quick insight into the political
climate of the time.

308   Schurmacher, Emile C.   "Spy Mission to Inchon"
Albert B. Tibbets. (editor).   Courage in Korea: Stories
of the Korean War.   Boston: Little, Brown, and Company,
1962.   140 - 162.
    A semi-fictionalized account of Lt. Eugene Clark
and his command's reconnaissance behind the lines at
Wolmi-do and Inchon harbor prior to the landing.

Films

BOOK

309   Butler, Lucius A. and Chaesoon T. Youngs. Films for
Korean Studies. Honolulu: Center for Korean Studies,
1978.
    Identifies more than one hundred and twenty 16mm
films on different aspects of the Korean War.   Lists
some films on the early phases of the war including
Inchon.

ARTICLES

310   Hulse, Ed.   "The Forgotten War"   Video Review
(November 1990) 57 - 59.
    A review of Korean War movies. Not only were there
very few such movies, but they were generally very poor.
The only movie directly related to Inchon, titled
Inchon, was produced by the Unification Church and was
not well received.

FILMS

311   <u>Combat Seals: America's Elite Warrior</u>.   Joseph
Dickstein Production, A Military Films, Inc., Quality
Video, 1991. 48 minutes.
     One of the few films available that deals with the
Underwater Demolition Teams during the Korean War, and
even this is pretty sketchy. The coverage of Inchon is
slight, but this is one of the few filmed accounts
available.

312   <u>Hell Over Korea: The First Forty Days</u>.   1985.
Ferde Grofe Films, Santa Monica, California.   100
minutes, 1/2 inch.
     Includes air combat films over Korea, primarily jet
footage.

313   <u>Inchon</u>. 1982. One Way Productions. Color, 102
minutes.   Starring Laurence Olivier and Jacqueline
Bissett.
     A big budget film paid for by the Unification
Church which is historically not very accurate, but
gives a view of what it "was like" to be there.

314   <u>Korea: The Forgotten War</u>. Video, 92 min, color,
b&w. Los Angeles, California: Fox Hills Video, 1987.
     Robert Stack narrates this fairly common account,
using rare archival combat footage without much
commentary. More interested with the Chinese period of
the war, but some early accounting.

315   <u>Korean Jet Aces</u>. 1989. Plymouth, Minnesota:
Simitar. VHS FUS and SIM 30 minutes.
     Archival gun-camera footage and interviews provide
interesting viewing.

316   <u>Korea, MacArthur's War</u>. Video, 54 min, b&w. MPI
Home Video, 1988.
     Examines the highly charged Korean War and
critically analyzes the reasons for it, as well as
General Douglas MacArthur's role in it.

317   Korea: The Unknown War. Produced by Austin Hoyt and Phillip Whitehead, Thames Television and WGBH-TV, Boston, 1990. 6 hours.
    Written by Jon Halliday and Bruce Cumings, the final version reflects a variety of opinions about the war. The Boston version is far easier on the Americans and Rhee than the British version and much of the films failure lies in the "Cold War world wide conspiracy thesis." While the film contains good footage of the Inchon landing the interpretation of events is limited in value.

318   Korean War: The Untold Story. Narrated by Loretta Swit. Pyramid Film And Video; Arnold Shapiro Producer, 34 min, b&w.
    This is a short but well produced account of the Korean War with some excellent footage of the Inchon landing. Several significant errors are apparent such as: "the marines were the first to fight in Korea," but well done.

319   The Korean War. Video, 30 min, b&w, color, GM-2585, Princeton, New Jersey: Films for the Humanities and Sciences.
    Covers the partitioning of Korea; the battles for Pusan, Inchon, and Seoul, General MacArthur's famous speeches, are all a significant part of this film presenting one last remaining moment of the East-West confrontation.

320   Motion Picture History of the Korean War. Video, 59 min, b&w. Marina Del Ray, California: Aviation Heritage Series. NFV, 1988.
    Covers all phases of the fighting from the outbreak of hostilities, on 25 June 1950, to the signing of the armistice on 27 July 1953. Inchon plays a dramatic part. Available from several different production companies.

321   Truman and the Korean War. The Truman Years.   18 min, b&w, TVT. D-3.
    Truman convened the Security Council of the United Nations to vote for intervention.

322   <u>US Navy SEAL's; World War II, Korea, Vietnam, Middle East, Grenada, Panama.</u>   Video by Quality Book, Paladin Press, Boulder, Col.   VHS color 90 minutes.

A somewhat dramatic account of the work of the navy's underwater teams at action in America's wars and semi-wars.   More instructive by the fact that they existed in Korea, and during the Inchon landing period, than by information presented.

APPENDIX

UNITED NATIONS FORCES OPERATION CHROMITE, 1950

Ground Forces

X (Tenth) Corps -- General

    50th Engineer Port Construction Company

    First Korean Marine Regiment

    1st Marine Division (Reinforced)

    KATUSA (8,652) assigned to 7th Infantry Division

    96th (155 mm) Field Artillery Battalion

    2nd Engineer Special Brigade

    7th Infantry Division (Reinforced)

    73rd Combat Engineer Battalion

    73rd Medium Tank Battalion

    65th Ordnance Ammunition Company

Naval Forces

Based on information in Anthony Farrar-Hockley, The British Part in the Korean War, Volume I, A Distant Obligation. London: HMSO, 1990. 512 pages, index, illustrations, maps, table, appendix.

Force Commander: Vice-Admiral A. D. Struble, USN
                  USS Rochester

Task Force 77 (Fast Carrier Group)
                  Rear Admiral E. C. Ewen, USN
                  USS Philippine Sea

        Carrier Division   USS Valley Forge
                                USS Boxer

        Cruiser Supports   USS Manchester
                                USS Worcester

        Destroyer Division   USS Eversole
                                USS Higsbee
                                USS James E. Kyes
                                USS Shelton
                                USS Chevalier
                                USS Theodore E. Chandler
                                USS Hanmer
                                USS Wiltsie
                                USS Hollitser
                                USS Frank Knox
                                USS McKean
                                USS Ozbourn
                                USS Fletcher
                                USS Radford

Task Force 79 (Service Squadron)
                  Captain B. L. Austin, USN

        6 oiler/tankers, 1 ammunition ship, 1
        refrigerated stores ship, 3 attack cargo ships,
        4 cargo ships, 2 destroyer tenders, 1 fleet tug,
        1 salvage vessel

Task Force 90   (Attack Force)
                Rear-Admiral J. H. Doyle, USN
                USS Mount McKinley

    Control Groups   Air and Shore

    Administrative Element

    Screening/Protective

        Destroyers   USS Bayonne
                                USS Evansville
                                USS Newport
                                USS Rowan
                                USS Southerland

        Frigates   La Grandiere (France)
                                HMS Mounts Bay
                                HMS Pukaki
                                HMS Tutira
                                HMS Whitesand Bay

                                2 patrol boats (ROK)
                                7 minesweepers (ROK)

    Landing Groups

        Advance landing: (3rd Bn, 5th Marines)
                                USS Fort Marion (LSD)
                                USS Horace A. Bass
                                USS Diachenko
                                USS Wantuck

        Balance: (1st Marine Division)
                                47 tank landing ships
                                1 medium landing ship
                                4 dock landing ships
                                9 attack transports
                                11 cargo ships
                                1 transport

                                (7th Infantry Division)
                                3 transports

4 transports (tracked)
12 merchant ships

(X Corps Troops)
1 transport
2 transports (tracked)
13 merchant ships

Tactical Air Support
Rear-Admiral R. W. Ruble, USN
USS Badoeng Strait

USS Sicily
USS Hanson
USS George K. Mackenzie
USS Ernest G. Small
USS Taussig

Gunfire Support Group
Rear-Admiral J. M. Higgins, USN
USS Toledo

Cruisers   USS Rochester
                   HMS Jamaica
                   HMS Kenya

Destroyers   USS De Haven
                   USS Mansfield
                   USS Lyman K. Swenson
                   USS Collett
                   USS Gurke
                   USS Henderson

Rocket Element
3 rocket-firing landing ships

Task Force 91   (Blockade and Covering Force)
Rear-Admiral W. G. Andrewes, RN
HMS Triumph

HMS Ceylon
HMS Athabaskan
HMS Bataan

HMS Cayuga
HMS Charity
HMS Cockade
Evertsen (Netherlands)
HMS Sioux
HMS Warramunga

3 ROK patrol boats
4 ROK minesweepers

Task Force 92   (X Corps)
            Major-General E. M. Almond, USA
            located with Rear-Admiral Doyle

Task Force 99 (Patrol/Reconnaissance Force)
            Rear-Admiral G. R. Henderson, USN

        seaplane tenders   USS Curtis
                           USS Gardiners Bay
                           USS Salisbury Sound

        aircraft units

        Patrol Squadron 6, 42, and 47

        Commonwealth units:
        88 and 289 Squadron, RAF

PERIODICALS REVIEWED

Aero Album
Aerospace Historian
Air Force
Airplane History
Airpower Historian
Airpower Journal
Air Trails
Air University Quarterly
America
American Aviation
American Aviation
    Historical
    Society Journal
American Heritage
American Historical
    View
American Journal of
    Psychiatry
American Legion
American Mercury
American Perspective
American Political
    Science Review
American Scholar
American Sociological
    Review

Annals of the American
    Academy of
    Political Social
    Science
Arizona and the West
Armed Forces and Society
Armor
Army
Army Digest
Army Information Digest
Army Logistician
Army Quarterly
Asian Affairs
Asian Defense Journal
Asian Survey
Asia Quarterly [Belgium]
Atlantic Monthly
Aviation History Society
    Journal
Aviation Week
Brassey's Annual: The
    Armed Forces Year-
    Book
Bulletin of Concerned
    Scholars
Business Week

Canadian Army Journal
Chaplain
China Quarterly
Christian Century
Collier's
Combined Forces Journal
Commentary
Comparative Political
    Studies
Conflict
Contemporary Review
Current History
Current Military
    Literature
Department of State
    Bulletin
Diplomatic History
Editor and Publisher
Education Public
Encounter
Engineers
Far Eastern Quarterly
Far Eastern Studies
Flying
Foreign Affairs
Foreign Policy Reports
Foreign Service Journal
Harper's
Historian
History
History Teacher
Illustrated London News
Infantry
Infantry School
    Quarterly
International Affairs
International
    Conciliation
International History
    Review
International Journal
International Review

    of Military
    History
International Studies
    Quarterly
Joint Perspectives
Journal of American
Journal of Asian Studies
Journal of Asiatic
    Studies
Journal of Contemporary
    Asia
Journal of Korean
Journal of Political and
    Military Sociology
Journal of Politics
Journal of the United
    Service
    Institution of
    India
Journalism Quarterly
Korea and World
    Affairs (South
    Korea)
Korean Affairs
Koreana Quarterly
Korean Journal
Korean Survey
Labor History
Leatherneck
Library Quarterly
Life
London News
Look
Marine Corps Gazette
Militaria
Military Affairs
Military Chaplain
Military Engineer
Military History Journal
Military Review
Military Surgeon
Modern China

Monthly Review
Nation
National Geographic
National Review
Naval Aviation News
Naval War College Review
New American Mercury
New Republic
New Statesman and Nation
New York Times Book
        Review
New York Times Magazine
Newsweek
Orbis
Pacific Affairs
Pacific Historical
        Review
Pacific Spectator
Pegasus
Pointer
Political Affairs
Political Science
        Quarterly
Presidential Studies
        Quarterly
Prologue
Public Administration
        Review
Public Interest
Public Opinion Quarterly
Quartermaster Review
Reporter
Review of Politics
Reviews in American
Rocky Mountain Social
        Science Journal
Royal Air Force
        Quarterly
Royal United Service
        Institute
Saturday Evening Post

Senior Scholastic
Signal
Soldiers
Studies in History and
        Society
Studies on the Soviet
        Union
Time
Twentieth Century
United National World
United Nations Bulletin
United Services and
        Empire Review
United States Armed
        Forces Medical
        Journal
United States Naval
        Institute
        Proceedings
US Air Force Historical
        Studies
US Air Service
US Army Aviation Digest
US News and World Report
Utah Historical
        Quarterly
Utah Historical Review
Video Review
Virginia Quarterly
        Review
Vital Speeches
Western Pennsylvania
        History
        Magazine
Wilson Quarterly
Wisconsin Magazine of
        History
World Affairs
World Today
Yale Review

AUTHOR INDEX

Unless noted, numbers refer to entries.

SUBJECT INDEX

Unless noted, numbers refer to entries.

About the Compiler

PAUL M. EDWARDS is Dean of the Graduate College of Park College in Parkville, Missouri, and founder and Executive Director of the Center for the Study of the Korean War in Independence, Missouri. His doctoral degree was in transatlantic history from the University of St. Andrews in Scotland. He is a specialist in Korean military and bibliographical history, and his most recent books include *The Pusan Perimeter, Korea, 1950: An Annotated Bibliography*, and *General Matthew B. Ridgway: An Annotated Bibliography*, both published in 1993 by Greenwood Press.